Wordworks

Wordworks

A Grammar Handbook
For
The Truly Desperate

Mary Collopy Southworth

The Williston Northampton School
Easthampton, Massachusetts

Longman
New York & London

Illustrations: Deborah Hamlet Putnam
Cover Design: G. Gordon Boice

Longman , 95 Church Street, White Plains, N.Y. 10601

Associated companies:
Longman Group Ltd., London
Longman Cheshire Pty, Melbourne
Longman Paul Pty., Auckland
Copp Clark Pitman, Toronto
Pitman Publishing Inc., New York

088334-192-1

6 7 8 9 10-MU-959493929

For Fran Dagbovie

and

all my students

Special thanks to the following for their efforts:

My husband, Tom Southworth, for his patience and encouragement

Emilie Conrad and William Lyons for personal and departmental support

CONTENTS

CLAUSES

FRAGMENTS

RUN-ONS

FREQUENT ERRORS

To the Student:

If you are truly desperate about grammar - or even just mildly anxious about it - WORDWORKS can help. This handbook presents grammar rules and how to use them in a clear, easy to read, entertaining style. The explanations and definitions are in plain language; you don't have to be an English teacher to figure them out.

Instead of tiny text crammed into a small space, large pages and open spacing provide a pleasing and manageable way to read the material. There is also plenty of room to complete the work right in the book.

There are no exercises about Madame Curie, Magellan's trip around the world or the person who invented the ironing board. The characters and experiences featured in the book are lively - and real. You can follow the adventures of several overweight cats and a mischievous boy named Adam while learning parts of speech and parts of sentence, or read about Dracula, dating misadventures and embarrassing moments while you work your way through phrases and clauses. Descriptions of chocolate desserts and delicious meals help you through a study of run-on and fragment sentences.

WORDWORKS helps you feel more comfortable with grammar because it is practical and easy to understand. It makes sense.

Wordworks

PARTS OF SPEECH

1. Nouns

2. Pronouns

3. Adjectives

4. Verbs

5. Interjections

6. Conjunctions

7. Adverbs

8. Prepositions

Nouns

Most grammar books define a noun as
1) a person
2) a place
3) a thing or object
4) a feeling
5) an idea

Examples:

cream	mess
butter	kitchen
chocolate	pan
sugar	job
Adam	anxiety

Note how these nouns are used in a paragraph:

Pudding is a favorite dish in our house, but last week <u>Adam</u> decided he wanted to try making it himself. This caused me some <u>anxiety</u> because the last time <u>Adam</u> used the <u>kitchen</u> he splattered cookie dough all over the walls. First, <u>Adam</u> melted <u>cream</u>, <u>butter</u>, and <u>sugar</u> in a <u>pan</u>. He added unsweetened <u>chocolate</u> to the mixture. Everything went well until he was faced with the <u>job</u> of transferring the mixture to a dish; the pan handle slipped from his hands, and the goop landed in a <u>mess</u> on the floor.

Exercise A
Directions: List at least <u>10</u> other nouns in the paragraph above:

_____   _____

_____   _____

_____   _____

_____   _____

_____   _____

Exercise B
Directions: Some of the nouns in the following paragraph have already been underlined; find as many other nouns as you can and underline them.

All children love their <u>rituals</u>, and Adam was no <u>exception</u>. Certain <u>things</u> had to be done in exactly the same <u>way</u> every day. I had to carry Adam down the stairs every <u>morning</u>; for some reason he didn't want his <u>feet</u> to touch the floor until we reached the kitchen. I was allowed to open his little box of <u>cereal</u>, but he insisted on pouring it in the bowl. <u>Sandwiches</u> were always cut in "triangles," never "<u>rectangles</u>." When he took a bath, Adam insisted on sitting in the <u>tub</u> until every drop of water had swirled down the drain. Before he could get into his bed at <u>night</u>, he had to break down what he called his "invisible <u>shield</u>." Night after night I waited until Adam waved his arms around, muttered some magic words, and finally announced that the "shield" was down.

Exercise C
Directions: Underline the nouns in the following paragraph:

When Adam was three years old, he fell in with bad company: the Conly boys from down the street. The Conly boys were notorious for the "pranks" they played on the neighbors. Once they fingerpainted the Andrews's car and a week later accidentally set fire to the Gallagher's garage. Adam, of course, thought the Conlys were the most exciting, wonderful boys he had ever met. They talked him into playing a game called "kitty capture." Adam's job was to lure various neighborhood cats into an old cardboard box. The Conly boys would fold the lids of the carton so that the animal could not escape, then plant the captured cat in a place where it would surely cause trouble. After the Boden's old tiger cat broke out of his box and beat up the Henderson's poodle, that was the end of "kitty capture." That was also the end of Adam's association with the Conlys!

Pronouns: The word "pro" comes from the Latin meaning "place of."
Pronouns take the place of nouns.

Pronouns are substitutes for nouns.

Example: Adam fed his Brussels sprouts to the cats.
noun

He fed his Brussels sprouts to the cats.
pronoun

List of common pronouns:

I	me	you	anything	few	other	myself
he	him	it	both	many	several	yourself
she	her	all	each	more	some	himself
we	us	another	either	most	somebody	herself
they	them	any	everybody	much	someone	itself
		anybody	everyone	none		ourselves
			everything	nobody		yourselves
				neither		themselves
				no one		who
				one		whose
						what
						which
						whom

Possessive Pronouns

Possessive pronouns tell who **owns** a noun.

Example: That's his squirt gun.
whose gun?   his

"I love you madly" is his usual opening line to all girls.
whose line?   his

It's their decision about our dinner plans.
whose decision?   what plans?
theirs   ours

My cats are named Amanda and Murphy.
whose cats?   my

Exercise D
Directions: Circle any pronouns or possessive pronouns in the sentences below.

1. "I will do anything for you," whispered the love-sick boy.

2. "You can start by taking your hands off my shoulder," answered his sarcastic girlfriend.

3. He tried other approaches: sending her flowers, writing a love letter every day, and singing outside her window.

4. Nothing worked. She wasn't interested in him because she thought he was clumsy and foolish.

5. On their last date, he knocked out her contact lens while angling for a kiss.

Exercise E
Directions: Look at the list of pronouns on page 6 and create a brief story using at least <u>5</u> pronouns:

_____

_____

_____

_____

_____

_____

_____

_____

Personal and Possessive Pronouns

Directions: Underline any pronouns.

1. Dating was not one of her favorite pastimes.

2. It usually involved some horribly humiliating or embarrassing experience for her.

3. Once at a drive-in movie her date forgot to remove the speaker that was hooked inside their car window.

4. The boy started the motor, his car shot forward, and the speaker crashed through the window and thumped to the ground.

5. Everybody turned to watch the embarrassed couple as they picked up shattered glass and the remains of the mangled speaker.

6. Another time she sat on a huge wad of bubble gum in the movie theatre.

7. Her date tried to pretend he wasn't with her.

8. Many awful moments took place in restaurants.

9. Everything had gone well until the main course arrived.

10. When she tried to slice her chicken, it slipped from the knife, slid across the table, and bounced to the floor.

Adjectives

Adjectives have one purpose: to describe nouns.

That's all they do, and there is no other part of speech that can describe a noun.

It's sometimes helpful to think of adjectives with arrows leading to the word they describe.

Example:

The fat, ugly, black cat slid off the couch.

   what kind of cat? =   fat cat

                          ugly cat

                          black cat

The gray blob on the rug is Amanda.

   what kind of blob: = gray blob

The green, grimy, gooey goop in the bowl is Adam's leftover pudding.

   what kind of goop? = green goop

                          grimy goop

                          gooey goop

The words "the," "a," and "an" are usually considered adjectives because they describe nouns. They are also referred to as "articles." Because some teachers want you to call them adjectives and others want you to call them articles, avoid the confusion and label them art./adj. This seems to satisfy nearly everyone.

art/adj.

the house

art/adj.

a likely story

art/adj.

an unusual story

Adjectives
Directions: Some of the nouns in the following sentences have been underlined. Find and label the adjectives that describe them.

1. The sad <u>lump</u> on the couch is Amanda, my oldest <u>cat</u>.

2. The fat black <u>cat</u> using Amanda for a pillow is Murphy.

3. Murphy has long black <u>hair</u> and a puffy <u>face</u>.

4. Murphy does not have normal cat <u>teeth</u>; she has long <u>fangs</u>.

5. I found Amanda in an old, run-down pet <u>store</u> in New York City.

6. <u>Amanda</u> is extremely jealous of Murphy but fond of her, too.

7. We do not have much <u>luck</u> keeping young <u>cats</u>.

8. Our kittens have broken their tiny <u>legs</u>, been run down by gigantic <u>cars</u>, and have fallen off wood <u>piles</u> and knocked unconscious.

9. I suspect the fiendish <u>Murphy</u> of plotting these frequent <u>accidents</u>.

10. <u>Murphy</u> and <u>Amanda</u> are delighted to have the couch to themselves.

Directions: Think of good adjectives that would describe the following nouns and place them in the spaces provided.

1. _____, _____ kid

2. _____, _____ dog

3. _____ dessert   4. _____ program

5. Amanda is _____.

Exercise F
Directions: 1) Underline and label each noun in the following sentences.
2) Underline each adjective and draw an arrow to the noun it describes.

1. The tall, thin man wearing the velvet cape is Dracula.

2. His oily, onion-colored eyes are fixated on your juicy flesh.

3. Dracula's glossy white skin is free from ugly scars or dark blemishes.

4. In the basement of his hideout, Dracula's ancient, rotting coffin can be found.

5. The oldest vampires live near Transylvania, but they have created thousands of other vampires who now live all over the world.

Exercise G
Directions: Using at least 5 of the adjectives listed below, make up a few sentences or a paragraph about anything you wish. Circle the adjectives and draw arrows to the nouns they describe.

gigantic	shabby	thick
deadly	shiny	sneaky
mossy	scaly	gloomy
delicious	rough	filthy

_____

_____

_____

_____

Adjectives and Nouns

It's good to remember that <u>the same word can be used as a different part of speech</u>. Words are not frozen. You'll run into trouble if you start saying to yourself, "Oh, that word is **always** a noun" or "That word is **always** an adjective."

<u>What a word "is" depends on how it is used.</u>
For example, the same word can be used as a noun OR an adjective.

Example: I love <u>spaghetti</u> made with fresh tomatoes.

             spaghetti = an object = noun

    I love <u>spaghetti</u> sauce made with sausage and peppers.

    What does the word "spaghetti" do in this sentence?

    It describes sauce.

    Sauce is a noun.

    What describes a noun?

    Only adjectives can describe nouns.

    What kind of sauce?
    Spaghetti sauce.

spaghetti = describes = adjective

Example: Adam smeared <u>chocolate</u> in his hair.

             thing = noun

    A rich <u>chocolate</u> sauce for ice cream is easy to make.

             describes = adjective

    Is the underlined word a **noun** or an **adjective**?

    <u>Cheese</u> can be used to enrich sauces and soups.

    I made a light <u>cheese</u> mixture to cover poached salmon.

    noun or adjective?

    I often use <u>cinnamon</u> when baking breads and cookies.

    noun or adjective?

    A light, smooth <u>cinnamon</u> cake is a delicious dessert.

    noun or adjective?

Exercise H
Directions: Use the words below in two sentences each: one sentence using the word as
a noun and another sentence using the word as an adjective.

1. strawberry _____

_____

_____

_____

2. chicken _____

_____

_____

_____

3. sugar _____

_____

_____

_____

4. school _____

_____

_____

_____

Verbs

Verbs can be divided into 2 categories:
1) "doing" verbs: **ACTION**
2) "do-nothing" being verbs: **LINKING**

1. In most sentences, someone or some thing is "doing" an action; that's what the sentence is all about.

   The "doing" verbs are words that are the <u>action</u>.

   Example: Amanda <u>raced</u> down the stairs and <u>crashed</u> into the door.

   If you get stuck, you can usually figure out what the verb is by asking, "what's happening?" or "what's doing?" in the sentence.

   Example: Amanda smacked Murphy on the head.
   Where's the action in this sentence? = Amanda <u>smacking</u> Murphy
   smacked = verb

   Example: Murphy rolled off the deck and crashed to the ground below.
   Where's the action? What's doing? What's happening? =
   rolling and crashing are what's happening
   rolled = verb
   crashed = verb

2. In other sentences, there isn't any action. People, events, or things are just **there,** existing but not doing much of anything.

   Verbs in these sentences are called "be" verbs or <u>linking verbs</u>.

Here is a list of common "be" or "linking" verbs:

appear	be	has been
become	being	have been
feel	am	should be
grow	is	would be
look	are	can be
remain	was	could be
seem	were	should have been
smell		
sound		
stay		
taste		

Linking verbs: It is worth taking another look at the linking verbs listed in the first column on page 15. These verbs confuse students because they imply more action than "is" or "are." They work as linking verbs because they link the subject with a word that describes the subject.

> **Example:** Bonzo <u>appears</u> silly.
>
> Bonzo = noun
>
> appears = verb
>
> silly = adjective

> Frog legs <u>smell</u> awful.
>
> legs = noun
>
> smell = verb
>
> awful = adjective

You can see the difference between <u>linking verbs</u> and <u>action verbs</u> in the following examples:

> **Example:** Adam <u>is</u> under the bed.   = linking verb
>
> Adam <u>sneaked</u> under the bed. = action verb

Exercise I

Directions: Underline every verb in the paragraph below.

He grew up in a small, dingy desert town in southern Arizona. His father was the town doctor, but the people were so poor they found it difficult to pay him for his services. They often found "gifts" on their back steps from those who were too poor to pay with money. Live chickens, home-baked bread, and hand-woven rugs were just a few of the items they received.

Nouns and Verbs

Remember how the same word can be used as a different part of speech? Sometimes the same word can be used as a noun <u>or</u> a verb, depending on how it is used in the sentence.

> **Example:** I <u>run</u> when I see Bonzo coming!
>
> We had a long <u>run</u> today and covered nearly four miles.

One is a noun and one is a verb, but how do you tell the difference?

Ask yourself:

1) Is someone <u>doing</u> the word? Then it has to be a verb.
2) Is the word an object, a thing by itself? Then it has to be a noun. Is it preceded by "a," "an," or "the," making it a thing? = noun.

I <u>run</u> when I see Bonzo coming!

Is someone "doing" the word?

Yes, "I" is doing the word; "I" is running.

run = verb

We had a long <u>run</u> today and covered nearly four miles.

Were we running? Or did we have <u>a</u> run?

We had <u>a</u> run.

The word <u>run</u> is a thing by itself.

Example: He let out a <u>scream</u> when he saw the shark fin.

I <u>scream</u> at the thought of a shark.

noun   or   verb?

Exercise J
Directions: Some of the verbs in the sentences below have already been underlined; underline the others.

1. The first year of Adam's life was not at all what I thought it <u>would be</u>.

2. He <u>cried</u> most of the day and played most of the night.

3. Everything he could grab went right into his mouth.

4. He even chewed on plants in the florist shop and <u>munched</u> on dry cat food.

5. Adam never got enough to eat.

6. One night I found him in a corner chomping loudly on a bunch of bananas!

7. He often <u>climbed</u> out of his crib in the middle of the night and turned on the television.

8. Adam loved wastebaskets.

9. Paper towels, chips of old soap, and old tubes of toothpaste were dumped on the floor and spread through the house.

10. He threw animal crackers at the cats' heads, <u>gnawed</u> on chair legs, and climbed the curtains.

Exercise K

Directions: Label the underlined words in the sentences below as either:

1) <u>noun</u>   2) <u>pronoun</u>   3) <u>adjective</u>   4) <u>verb</u>

*Remember to label the words "a," "the," and "an" as <u>art./adj.</u>
*Remember to note how the word is used.

1. A <u>delicious</u> <u>meal</u> <u>can be made</u> from rice, <u>tender</u> meat marinated in a <u>vinegar</u> broth, bay leaves, onions, and a little saffron.

2. <u>Fresh</u> spices and herbs are <u>excellent</u> <u>aids</u> to fine cooking.

3. A <u>good</u> <u>beginning</u> to <u>a</u> <u>special</u> meal is a <u>clear</u>, <u>spicy</u>, <u>tomato</u> <u>soup</u> <u>made</u> with <u>fresh</u> vegetables, basil, and tarragon.

4. <u>Chocolate</u> cream <u>pie</u> is another delicious dessert that is made quickly and easily. Chocolate, a cup of honey, and a half <u>cup</u> of cream <u>are</u> the <u>main</u> <u>ingredients</u>.

5. A rich, <u>fudge</u>, ice cream sundae pie is a great summer dessert.

6. Platte County Pie is made with butter, sugar, chocolate chips, whipped cream, and <u>crushed</u> <u>walnuts</u>.

7. <u>Chocolate</u> brownies <u>taste</u> better when you <u>use</u> imported vanilla extract in the batter.

8. <u>Sticky</u>, <u>gooey</u>, <u>chocolate</u> cookies <u>will stay</u> fresh a little longer if <u>you</u> <u>put</u> a small piece of an apple core in the cookie jar.

9. Any <u>chicken</u> <u>dish</u> will taste better if the meat has been soaked in cooking sherry, peppers, and onions.

10. <u>Barbequed</u> chicken <u>should be flamed</u> first over <u>high</u> heat; this seals in the juices and <u>keeps</u> the meat from drying out.

Review: Parts of Speech, Part One

Directions: Identify the underlined words as noun, pronoun, adjective, or verb.

1. The <u>decade</u> of the 1960's <u>produced</u> many <u>fads</u>, including <u>hair</u> ironing, <u>white</u> lipstick, and mini-skirts.

2. <u>Ragged</u> jeans, scuffy <u>loafers</u>, an old army jacket and <u>an</u> <u>Indian</u> bead headband <u>were</u> part of <u>my</u> <u>usual</u> <u>outfit</u> in the late 60's.

3. In 1964 the Beatles <u>visited</u> <u>the</u> United States for the <u>first</u> time and <u>caused</u> havoc in many American homes.

4. <u>My</u> <u>best</u> friend and <u>I</u> put bowls over our <u>heads</u> <u>to use</u> as <u>guides</u> for cutting our hair like the Beatles.

5. Our <u>parents</u> were <u>furious</u> and "grounded" us for a month.

6. Many parents <u>disliked</u> the <u>new</u>, loud music of the 1960's.

7. I kept my <u>supply</u> of music in a <u>brown</u> paper bag at my friend's house.

8. <u>Paper</u> dresses, white stockings, and <u>ankle</u> bracelets were very <u>popular</u> in those <u>days</u>.

9. A well dressed boy wore a <u>madras</u> shirt, chino pants, white <u>socks</u>, and penny <u>loafers</u>.

Interjections

Interjections are the easiest part of speech. They are expressions used to show feelings and have no relationship, in terms of grammar, to the rest of the sentence.

Example: Ouch

Quiet!

Oh, Boy!

At last!

Ugh!

Yuck!

Wow!

Conjunctions

The word conjunction comes from the Latin meaning "something that joins."

Conjunctions are words that join words or groups of words.

Here's a list of common conjunctions:

and	nor
but	for
or	yet

Example: I love cake <u>and</u> cookies.

We hopped over the fence, <u>but</u> the principal was waiting on the other side.

You can eat Krazy Krunchies <u>or</u> Midnight Fudge Bars.

Adverbs

Adverbs can do three things:

> 1) describe verbs
>
> 2) describe adjectives
>
> 3) describe other adverbs

Adverbs usually answer these questions:

> 1) where?
>
> 2) when?
>
> 3) how?
>
> 4) why?
>
> 5) how long?
>
> 6) how much?

Adverbs that describe or modify verbs:

Example: Adam ate quickly.

What is the verb in the sentence?

Ate is the verb.

Ate how?

Ate <u>quickly</u>.

> quickly = adverb

Adam ate quickly.

Example: Bonzo read quietly.

What is the verb in the sentence?

Read is the verb.

Read how?

Read <u>quietly</u>.

> quietly = adverb

Bonzo read quietly.

Exercise L: Part One
Directions: 1) Find the verb in each sentence.
2) Find and label the adverb describing the verb.
3) Draw an arrow from the adverb to the verb it describes.

1. Amanda, the old cat, slept soundly.

2. Adam sneaked silently through the deserted house.

3. The vampire waited patiently for his next victim.

4. Murphy, the fat cat, quietly squished the baby mouse and bit off its head.

5. Adam slurped noisily on his chocolate fudge soda.

6. Bonzo escaped and ran fast!

7. The creamy caramel cookies melted slowly in his hand.

Adverbs that describe verbs
Directions: Some of the verbs in the following sentences have been underlined; find the
adverbs that describe them.

1. The two boys <u>crept</u> quietly through the dark.

2. Dracula <u>hissed</u> violently when he saw their pale faces.

3. The old vampire hastily <u>transformed</u> himself into a wolf and <u>fled</u> quickly through the
Carpathian mountains.

4. The boys <u>peered</u> cautiously into the castle.

5. Suddenly, huge purple hands <u>grabbed</u> the smallest boy by the throat.

Directions: Make up <u>adverbs</u> for the spaces provided.

1. The boy screamed _____.

2. Adam watched _____ from his place on the couch.

3. Frankenstein grabbed my arm _____.

4. Erin _____ smashed her little sister's finger.

5. Adam ate _____ and _____.

Adverbs that describe or modify other Adverbs:

Example: She spoke too quietly.

What is the verb in the sentence?

Spoke is the verb.

Spoke how?

Spoke quietly.

quietly = adverb

How quietly?

Too quietly.

too = adverb

adv.   adv.

She spoke too quietly.

1. ADVERBS describe VERBS

2. ADVERBS describe ADJECTIVES

3. ADVERBS describe other ADVERBS

Exercise L: Part Two

Directions: 1) Find the verb in each sentence.

2) Find and label the adverb describing the verb.

3) Draw an arrow from the adverb to the verb it describes.

1. Amanda sleeps soundly on the porch every morning.

2. I moved immediately.

3. He sat here.

4. We will finish the pie soon.

5. Let's go there.

Adverbs that describe adverbs
Directions: 1) Locate the verb.
                2) Find and label the adverb that describes the verb.
                3) Find and label the adverb that describes another adverb.

1. The bug squeaked so horribly we winced in disgust.

2. The spider crept very cautiously on the window ledge.

3. Lilly was spying somewhat secretly behind the curtain.

4. She squished the spider so thoroughly it looked like black jam.

5. Another intended victim scuttled away too quickly and one spider life was saved.

6. During a temper tantrum over chicken soup, Lilly stamped her feet so hard she broke the buckles on her patent leather shoes.

7. Lilly eats incredibly fast.

8. The first dozen cupcakes slid down quite easily.

Exercise M
Directions: 1) Find the adjective in each sentence.
2) Find and label the adverb describing the adjective.
3) Draw an arrow from the adverb to the adjective it describes.

1. Adam is an unusually sneaky person!

2. Trevor admired his amazingly beautiful row of Hot Wheels cars.

3. Amanda gave Murphy a very nasty look.

4. We munched on the extremely delicious fried cheese.

5. Bonzo made a completely dumb remark about frogs, spiders, and girls.

Exercise N
Directions: 1) Find the verb in each sentence.
2) Find the adverb that describes the verb.
3) Find and label the adverb that describes the adverb.
4) Draw an arrow from the adverb to the other adverb it describes.

1. I saw that movie rather recently.

2. Bonzo's weight has increased rather dramatically this year.

3. If Adam climbs out of his window very quietly, I can't hear him.

4. The boys did extremely well in the match against their arch rival.

Adverbs that describe adjectives
Directions: Find and label the adverbs that describe adjectives.

1. Adam has amassed an unusually large collection of useless toys.

2. The trail through Adam's room is fairly hazardous.

3. Marbles, pieces of abandoned projects, and baseball cards are scattered across the extremely cluttered room.

4. Adam's closet is terribly crowded with old kites, a Mickey Mouse stool, Boston Bruins banners, and ancient cowboy hats.

5. Cleaning Adam's room is a very tedious experience.

Directions: Provide an adverb in the space that describes the adjective.

1. a _____ horrible meal

2. a _____ bad day

3. _____ disgusting mess

4. _____ sticky lump

5. _____ scary movie

Exercise O

Directions: 1) Underline and label each adverb in the sentences below.

2) Draw an arrow to the word the adverb describes.

3) Label the word the adverb describes as a verb, adjective, or adverb.

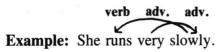

verb adv. adv.

Example: She runs very slowly.

adv.   adj.

The incredibly handsome boy had fine skin and blue eyes.

1. The boys sneaked silently through the halls.

2. They were on a most dangerous mission: to confiscate the ice cream sandwiches in

   the cafeteria.

3. They checked constantly to make sure a teacher wasn't around.

4. Their shoes creaked so loudly on the wooden floorboards that they were forced to

   continue in bare feet.

5. They entered the cafeteria and found themselves in an incredibly embarrassing position:

   Mr. Doolittle had caught on to their plan and was waiting patiently for their arrival.

Exercise P

Directions: 1) Write a sentence in which an adverb describes a verb.

2) Write a sentence in which an adverb describes an adjective.

3) Write a sentence in which an adverb describes an adverb.

_____

_____

_____

Catching Up

Exercise Q
Directions: Write a few sentences about any topic you wish, making sure to include at
least one adjective, one adverb, one conjunction, and one interjection; underline and label.

_____

_____

_____

_____

_____

_____

Exercise R
Directions: Identify the underlined parts of speech as either noun, pronoun, adjective,
verb, conjunction, interjection, or adverb.

1. <u>Murphy</u> is an <u>unbelievably</u> <u>lazy</u> cat. We call <u>her</u> "The Slug."

2. <u>She</u> <u>and</u> Amanda <u>quarrel</u> over the <u>cat</u> food.

3. Murphy <u>moves</u> <u>so</u> <u>slowly</u> she's difficult to identify as a <u>live</u> object.

4. <u>Ugh</u>! Murphy licked <u>me</u> on the nose!

5. <u>Chocolate</u> mousse <u>is</u> <u>very</u> <u>easy</u> to make.

Prepositions

1. Prepositions usually explain a position or place.

The word "position" is inside the word "preposition" and might help you to remember what prepositions are.

Prepositions

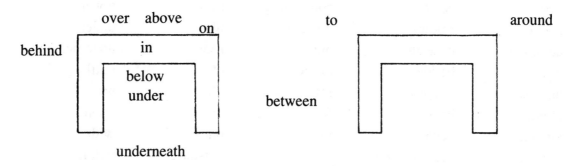

2. Prepositions always come in phrases.

<u>in</u> the drawer	<u>between</u> the two tables
<u>under</u> the table	<u>behind</u> the ugly table
<u>on</u> the table	<u>above</u> the table

PREP. <u>around</u> the corner	prepositional phrase
PREP. <u>except</u> Bonzo	prep. phrase
PREP. <u>after</u> midnight	prep. phrase
PREP. <u>beyond</u> the Twilight Zone	prep. phrase

In the opinion of some students, "Memorizing prepositions is a classic drag," but you'll save yourself trouble and time later on if you commit these to memory now.

List of common prepositions

aboard	before	by	inside	to
about	behind	concerning	into	toward
above	below	down	like	under
across	beneath	during	near	underneath
after	beside	except	of	until
against	besides	for	off	up
along	between	from	on	upon
among	beyond	in	onto	with
around	but (meaning		outside	within
at	except)		over	without
			past	
			since	
			through	

Exercise S

Directions: 1) Circle the preposition.
2) Underline the prepositional phrase.

Example: Amanda socked Murphy (on) the nose.

(In) the beginning (of) Adam's favorite story, an alligator falls (off) a roof.

1. You'll find the fudge and the brownies in the refrigerator.

2. I found Adam's homework stuffed under his bed.

3. When Murphy and Amanda are afraid, they hide behind the bedroom door.

4. Murphy likes sleeping inside the mattress on cold days.

"TO" as a **PREPOSITION** and as a **VERB**

Remember how words aren't frozen and can be used as different parts of speech? But on the lookout for the word "to." It can be used as a preposition, and it can also be used as a verb. Students get used to identifying "to" as a preposition and then forget that it can be part of a verb as well.

How do you tell the difference?

1. "to" as a preposition will be in a prepositional phrase

I will take Adam <u>to the toy store</u>.

2. "to" as a verb will be followed by a verb

I suppose I have <u>to take</u> you!

He likes <u>to entertain</u> his classmates by imitating the faculty.

I started <u>to scream</u> when I saw the hand on the window pane.

Part of a verb or a preposition?

1. I am willing to extend the deadline date for your compositions.

2. It's difficult not to believe everything you read.

3. It's going to be impossible to go to the store today.

Prepositions
Directions: The prepositions are underlined; find the prepositional phrases.

1. Suddenly a decapitated mouse landed <u>on</u> my doorstep.

2. The mouse heads <u>on</u> the front steps were gifts <u>from</u> the cats.

3. Murphy crammed the squashed mouse <u>into</u> her mouth.

4. I created a gruesome story <u>for</u> Adam <u>about</u> mouse heads.

5. The sneaky child hid his dirty clothes <u>behind</u> the shoes <u>in</u> the closet.

Prepositions
Directions: Underline the preposition and circle the prepositional phrase.

1. Dracula lunged for his throat.

2. Adam bounced off the bed and landed on his head.

3. The chocolate ribbon cake on the table in the dining room is for you.

4. The sophisticated, suave children in this classroom are my students.

5. Adam and Gavin slid down the snow-covered hill on cafeteria trays.

Exercise T
Directions: 1) Circle the preposition.
                 2) Underline the prepositional phrase.

1. Dracula leaves his victims before daylight.

2. It is not true that vampires can slip through keyholes, but they can turn themselves into cats, bats, or wolves.

3. A vampire does not cast a reflection in a mirror.

4. Dracula leaned toward his beautiful victim and bit her soft, fleshy neck.

5. Frankenstein is buried beneath mounds of snow in the Arctic.

6. The creator of this horrible monster was Victor Frankenstein.

7. The Werewolf is dead from the shot of a silver bullet.

8. We put fresh roses and a wreath of garlic on the door to protect us against vampires.

9. The vampire has been stabbed with a wooden stake, but to be safe we should place garlic in his mouth and cut off his head.

Parts of Speech
Directions: Identify the underlined word as interjection, adjective, conjunction, adverb, or preposition.

1. It was <u>very</u> <u>difficult</u> for me to sneak out <u>of</u> the house wearing my mini-skirt.

2. I had to creep <u>very</u> <u>quietly</u> <u>down</u> the back stairs and make a dash for the car when my mother wasn't looking.

3. The early fads <u>of</u> the 1960's were <u>considerably</u> <u>different</u> from those that appeared later <u>in</u> the decade.

4. During the early 60's, boys <u>often</u> dyed their hair white-blond and strapped surfboards <u>to</u> the roofs <u>of</u> their cars to imitate the Beach Boys.

5. Long, puffy hair was <u>very</u> popular for girls.

6. To achieve the right effect, girls rolled their hair <u>in</u> gigantic empty orange juice cans.

7. <u>Ouch</u>! cried Trevor, as he squished his thumb <u>in</u> the drawer.

8. Adam <u>and</u> Gavin laughed <u>hysterically</u> when Trevor ate the tamale pie that was <u>too</u> <u>hot</u> <u>for</u> him.

9. Adam <u>and</u> Gavin found several interesting ways to tease Trevor, <u>but</u> the <u>most</u> <u>effective</u> method was to put chocolate chip cookies in the clothes hamper <u>and</u> lure Trevor inside.

10. Trevor found the thought of crunchy, <u>delicious</u> cookies irresistible, and <u>usually</u> climbed <u>inside</u> the hamper.

Exercise U
Directions: Identify the underlined parts of speech as either:

1) noun
2) pronoun
3) adjective
4) verb
5) interjection
6) conjunction
7) adverb
8) preposition

1. I'd like <u>to make</u> <u>chocolate</u> cake, <u>but</u> <u>I</u> have run out <u>of</u> the <u>main</u> ingredients, chocolate and nutmeg.

2. A <u>creamy</u> angel food cake <u>is</u> not <u>too</u> difficult <u>to make</u>. First bake the cake <u>slowly</u>, then <u>top</u> with whipped cream <u>and</u> sprinkles.

3. <u>Ordinary</u> chocolate chips, a little whipped cream, <u>a</u> drop <u>of</u> vanilla extract, and <u>six</u> eggs will make a <u>wonderfully</u> <u>easy</u> <u>mousse</u>.

4. An elegant <u>Easter</u> dinner is made even <u>more</u> special when glazed ham is the <u>main</u> course.

5. Boil the ham <u>very</u> <u>slowly</u> <u>for</u> half an hour. <u>Remove</u> the ham, place on a rack and cover <u>with</u> a sauce made <u>from</u> brown sugar, cloves, and jelly.

6. A <u>good</u> trick <u>to remember</u> when making chocolate chip cookies is <u>to melt</u> the butter <u>separately</u> before adding <u>to</u> the sugar.

Exercise V
Directions: Identify the part of speech of each underlined word:

1. The vampire, who had <u>incredible</u> <u>strength</u>, <u>hurled</u> the body <u>across</u> the room.

2. The boy <u>discovered</u> Dracula's coffin, <u>threw</u> open the lid, and <u>plunged</u> a <u>wooden</u> stake <u>in</u> the vampire's heart. For an instant, the vampire's eyes fluttered open in terror.

3. "Let <u>me</u> in," pleaded the vampire, "I'm hungry."

4. The handsome vampire <u>smiled</u> <u>longingly</u> <u>at</u> my neck.

Exercise W
Directions: Identify the part of speech of each underlined word:

During <u>the</u> <u>two</u> <u>years</u> <u>I</u> lived in <u>New York</u>, I <u>must have encountered</u> <u>every</u> nut in

the city. <u>Some</u> of my <u>worst</u> <u>experiences</u> took place on the <u>bus</u> <u>ride</u> <u>to</u> work. Once an old

man <u>took</u> the seat next to mine and began <u>to carry</u> on a <u>very</u> <u>loud</u> and <u>interesting</u>

<u>conversation</u> <u>with</u> the box <u>he</u> was holding in <u>his</u> hands. I sneaked a <u>look</u> into the box: it

was filled with dirt. Another time <u>a</u> <u>rather</u> <u>young</u> and beautiful woman <u>threw</u> her shoes

<u>out</u> the <u>bus</u> <u>window</u>, claiming they were full of worms. Once a man in a <u>business</u> suit

grabbed me by the <u>coat</u> lapels and told me that it <u>was</u> my fault his teeth had fallen out.

I decided <u>to abandon</u> the bus and take the <u>subway</u> to work; it would be <u>more</u> <u>safe</u>!

Exercise X
Directions: Identify the part of speech of each underlined word:

<u>Some</u> <u>of</u> my <u>worst</u> experiences as <u>an</u> <u>adolescent</u> involved driving. <u>Two</u> weeks after I got my license, I <u>slid</u> the car on a <u>patch</u> of ice and <u>spun</u> <u>into</u> a ditch. This <u>bruised</u> my <u>confidence</u> somewhat, <u>and</u> soon my approach to driving <u>was</u> one <u>of</u> fear, <u>panic</u>, and <u>stupidity</u>. Once in the <u>early</u> spring of my junior year in high school I <u>borrowed</u> my father's <u>enormous</u> Lincoln. I drove to my parents' farm, where I wanted <u>to inspect</u> a lake that had been <u>newly</u> stocked with fish. <u>Foolishly</u>, I drove to the water's edge. When I <u>returned</u> from <u>my</u> walk, I discovered that the <u>heavy</u> car had sunk into the soft, squishy, <u>spring</u> mud. It took two wreckers all day <u>to remove</u> the car.

*   *   *

My father <u>warned</u> me <u>repeatedly</u> <u>about</u> being careful when I backed the car out of the <u>narrow</u> garage. <u>His</u> lectures made me <u>so</u> <u>nervous</u> that I began to open the car door a little each time I backed out. I thought <u>this</u> was a <u>clever</u> way <u>to make</u> <u>sure</u> I had enough space. One day I opened the door <u>too</u> <u>far</u> and smashed <u>into</u> the side of the garage. Panicked, I stepped on, instead of off, the gas pedal and zoomed out of the driveway. The <u>car</u> <u>door</u> ripped right off.

PARTS OF SENTENCE

1. Predicate nominative

2. Predicate adjective

3. Direct object

4. Indirect object

5. Object of the preposition

6. Correct Use of Pronouns as Complements

Parts of Sentence: Complements

Parts of Sentence: Subjects, Predicates (verbs), and **Complements**

Just when you've mastered <u>parts of speech</u>, along comes someone who tells you there's yet another way to identify words: <u>as parts of sentences</u>.

Not all parts of speech will be used as parts of sentence. However, when a word is part of a sentence, it is <u>still</u> a part of speech.

Example:

Parts of Sentence:	**subject**	**verb**			**D.O.**
	Murphy	ate	the	chocolate	cake.
Parts of Speech:	**noun**	**verb**	**art/adj.**	**adj.**	**noun**

<u>subjects</u>: are always nouns or pronouns
    <u>verbs</u>: are either action (run, shout, jump) or linking verbs (is, are, was, etc.)
<u>complements</u>: are either nouns, pronouns, or adjectives

Complements are used to complete the meaning of some sentences. There are two kinds of complements:

Subject Complements and **Object Complements**

predicate nominative (PN) direct object (DO)
predicate adjective (PA) indirect object (IO)
object of the preposition (OP)

Subject Complements:

<u>predicate nominative</u> — always a noun or a pronoun

1) follows   2) names or explains
   the   the
   linking   subject
   verb

subject = predicate nominative

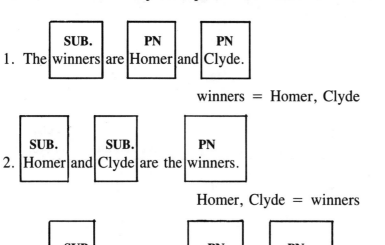

1. The [SUB. winners] are [PN Homer] and [PN Clyde].

winners = Homer, Clyde

2. [SUB. Homer] and [SUB. Clyde] are the [PN winners].

Homer, Clyde = winners

3. The [SUB. names] of my cats are [PN Murphy] and [PN Amanda].

names = Murphy, Amanda

4. [SUB. It] was a very cold [PN day].

it = day

5. [SUB. Bonzo] is a [PN nerd].

Bonzo = nerd

Predicate Nominatives

Directions: The subjects of the following sentences are underlined.
Find and label the predicate nominative in each sentence.
The predicate nominative will:

        a. follow the linking verb

        b. be a noun

        c. name or explain the subject

1. <u>It</u> is a gruesome nightmare.

2. The <u>lumps</u> of clothes on the chair became slimy monsters.

3. The <u>jackets</u> in the closet are silent, deadly soldiers.

4. The <u>carpet</u> is a sea of sharks.

5. My <u>blanket</u> was a nest of snakes.

Directions: Find and label the predicate nominatives.

1. Bonzo is my best friend.

2. Pastries, chocolate, and potato chips are my favorite junk foods.

3. The creature in the stove is a mouse.

4. The cats and the mouse are buddies.

5. Robert and Noah were the students involved in the dissected frog scandal.

Exercise A: predicate nominatives
Directions: 1) Find and underline the linking verb.
           2) Circle and label the subject.
           3) Circle and label the predicate nominative.

1. Mr. Doolittle was my favorite teacher.

2. One of his worst habits is biting his toenails.

3. Helter Skelter is the terrifying story of the Charles Manson murders.

4. The chicken thieves were Amanda and Murphy; they leaped on the table and made away with our dinner.

5. The students hiding under the teacher's desk are Hans and David.

Exercise B: predicate nominatives
Directions: Using the list of linking verbs below, write five sentences that contain a subject and a predicate nominative. Underline the verb, circle the subject, and circle and label the predicate nominative.

         be   am   is   are   was   were

_____

_____

_____

_____

_____

Subject Complements:

predicate adjective — always an adjective

1) follows the linking verb

2) describes the subject

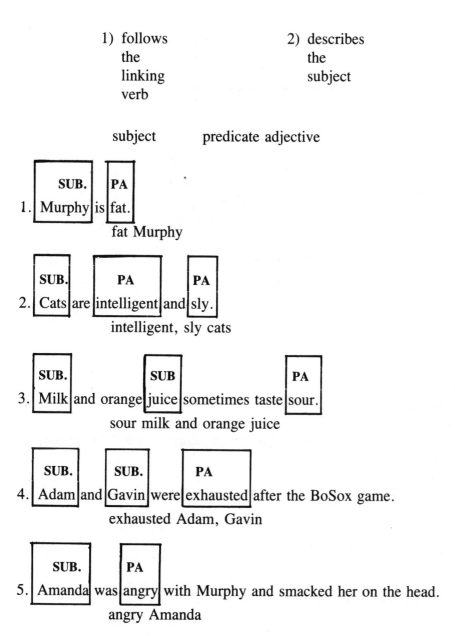

subject   predicate adjective

1. | SUB. Murphy | is | PA fat. |
fat Murphy

2. | SUB. Cats | are | PA intelligent | and | PA sly. |
intelligent, sly cats

3. | SUB. Milk | and orange | SUB juice | sometimes taste | PA sour. |
sour milk and orange juice

4. | SUB. Adam | and | SUB. Gavin | were | PA exhausted | after the BoSox game.
exhausted Adam, Gavin

5. | SUB. Amanda | was | PA angry | with Murphy and smacked her on the head.
angry Amanda

Predicate Adjectives

Note: There is a difference between regular adjectives and predicate adjectives. Remember that to be a predicate adjective, the adjective has to <u>follow</u> a linking verb.

Example:

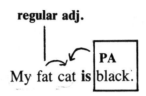

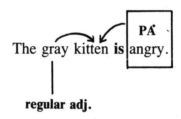

Exercise C: predicate adjectives
Directions: 1) Find and underline the linking verb.
  2) Circle and label the subject.
  3) Circle and label the predicate adjective and draw an arrow to the subject it describes.

1. The tall, thin boy was very handsome.

2. Adam is cranky and crabby today.

3. Dracula's castle is dark, dank, and spooky.

4. Dracula's eyes were wild with desire for her soft, fleshy neck.

Predicate Adjective

Directions: The subjects in the following sentences are underlined. Find and label the predicate adjectives in each sentence.

Predicate adjectives will:
1. follow the linking verb
2. be adjectives
3. describe the subject

1. The squashed <u>squirrel</u> smelled horrible.

2. <u>Trevor</u> was delighted with the batch of peanut butter cookies.

3. Seasoned snake <u>meat</u> is tasty and nutritious.

4. The fried frog <u>legs</u> were greasy and delicious.

5. This raw <u>liver</u> is too salty!

Directions: Find and label the predicate adjectives.
1. Students are often intelligent and entertaining.

2. Gavin was furious when Trevor colored his sneakers with the green magic marker.

3. Susan is nervous about her date with Bonzo.

4. Count Dracula's dinner tasted delicious!

5. Perhaps Bonzo only <u>seems</u> ridiculous.

Subject Complements: <u>predicate nominatives</u> and <u>predicate adjectives</u>

Sometimes it is difficult to tell the difference between a predicate adjective and a predicate nominative when it's not clear if the word after the linking verb is describing <u>or</u> naming the subject.

For example, in the sentence "Bonzo is a nerd," some kids will insist that "nerd" has to be a predicate adjective because it describes Bonzo. In a way, that is correct, but "nerd" is not an adjective.

How do you tell the difference?

1. Ask yourself: Is the word following the linking verb a noun or an adjective? If it is a noun, it has to be a PN. If it is an adjective, it has to be a PA.

2. Ask yourself: Is the word the <u>same thing</u> as the subject, or does it merely describe the subject? If the subject and the word are the same, it is a PN. If the word just describes, it is a PA.

Example:

1. Jacob <u>is</u> the <u>clown</u> in our class.

   Jacob and clown are interchangeable; they are the same thing. Clown is a PN.

2. Trevor <u>was</u> <u>angry</u> when Gavin tied his shoelaces together.

   Are "Trevor" and "angry" interchangeable? Are they the same thing? No; "angry" just describes Trevor and is a PA.

Predicate Nominatives and Predicate Adjectives

Directions: Find and label the predicate adjectives and the predicate nominatives.

Remember to look for linking verbs!

1. Lilly is the girl who squashes bugs with her thumb.

2. Adam was frightened when I told him Dracula was lurking outside his bedroom window.

3. Amanda is such a foolish cat! She ran into a closed window as she was attacking a bird and knocked herself unconscious.

4. Rodney is the suave opposite of the clumsy Bonzo.

5. Dudley and Bonzo were thrilled when they discovered the key to the cafeteria.

6. Barry and Rocky were old family dogs.

7. Barry was a dumpy overweight border collie.

8. Rocky was a slim golden retriever that became fat after a few months in our house.

9. Barry was spoiled and very jealous of Rocky.

10. The silly collie was outraged when Rocky became a member of the family.

Object Complements: are always nouns or pronouns; object complements are people or things.

<u>direct object</u>, <u>indirect object</u>, <u>object of the preposition</u>

Direct Object: usually defined as a "word that receives the action of a verb" in most grammar books

A direct object is the word that tells <u>to what</u> or <u>to whom</u> the action has happened.

Example:

          v.
1. Murphy smacked <u>Adam</u> on the head with her paw.
    smacked whom?   Adam
        Adam = direct object

         v.
2. The ninth graders ate blueberry <u>pie</u>, <u>pizza</u>, and <u>ice cream</u>.
    ate what?   pie, pizza, ice cream
        pie, pizza, ice cream = direct objects

Indirect Object: usually defined as the word that tells "to whom" or "for whom" the action of the verb is done

An indirect object is the noun or pronoun that comes <u>before</u> the direct object and tells us the person (sometimes the thing) the action is for.

Example:

1. Murphy gave Adam a smack on the head.
   gave what?   Smack = direct object
   to whom?   Adam = indirect object

      v.   IO   **DO**
2. We <u>baked</u> <u>Bonzo</u> a chocolate <u>cake</u>.
   baked what?   cake = **DO**
   for whom?   Bonzo = **IO**

Note: If you have a direct object, you may or may not have an indirect object.

If you have an indirect object, you will <u>always</u> have a direct object.

Object of the Preposition: is the noun at the end of the prepositional phrase

Example:

prep. phrase

1. The half-eaten apple was left <u>on the counter</u>.

    on = prep.

    on what? = Counter

    counter = object of prep.

OP

2. Bonzo looked up Edna's name <u>in the telephone book</u>.

    in = prep.

    in where? = book

    book = **OP**

Direct Objects and Indirect Objects

Directions: Identify the underlined words as direct objects or indirect objects

1. My father lectured <u>me</u> about my wild hair, messy room, and collection of rock music.

2. My brother wrote <u>me</u> a <u>letter</u> about his exciting life in Hong Kong.

3. Hong Kong had several strange <u>murders</u> last year.

4. One person killed a <u>man</u> using barbeque sticks!

5. The dean of students gave <u>Dudley</u> a warning about climbing out of the study hall window.

6.   My sister enjoys buying <u>Adam</u> unusual <u>toys</u>.

7.   Last year she bought <u>Adam</u> a snake water pistol, an electric hand <u>buzzer</u>, and a plastic witch <u>nose</u>.

8.   Adam squirted <u>Murphy</u>!

9.   Murphy gave <u>Adam</u> a disgusted <u>look</u> and lumbered away.

10.   Gavin sold <u>Adam</u> his snapping alligator hand <u>puppet</u>.

Exercise D: object complements

Directions: Label the DOs, IOs, or OPs in the following sentences.

1.   Adam gave <u>Murphy</u> and <u>Edna</u> a juicy <u>kiss</u>.

2.   Adam locked <u>Gavin</u> and <u>Trevor</u> in the <u>bathroom</u>.

3.   During long car rides, my husband entertains <u>me</u> by singing, doing <u>imitations</u>, and making foolish <u>remarks</u> about the people in passing <u>cars</u>.

Exercise E: object complements

Directions: 1) Underline the linking verbs.
2) Find any PAs or PNs; circle and label them.
3) Draw an arrow to the subject they explain or describe.

1. Amanda is old and dumb, but I love her anyway.

2. Dracula smiled, but his teeth looked blood-stained.

3. Bonzo is an incredible bore.

4. Gavin and Trevor are my step-sons.

5. My favorite meal is baked shrimp in garlic sauce.

Complements

Directions: Label the underlined words as PA, PN, DO, IO, or OP. You have been given some hints!

                  lv   **action verb**

1. Lemon mousse is <u>easy</u> to make, so I didn't mind that Tyler ate four <u>pieces</u>.

                  linking verb   **prep.**

2. The noisy boys were <u>Max</u> and <u>Greg</u>; they were on the <u>fire escape</u>.

                  action verb

3. Adam and Gavin gave <u>Trevor</u> the "<u>cookie treatment</u>."

        lv

4. Trevor was <u>wild</u> with <u>excitement</u>.

                action verb   **prep.**   **prep.**

5. The older boys told <u>Trevor</u> the <u>story</u> about the magic <u>chips</u> in the <u>cookies</u>.

                prep.   **lv**   **action verb action verb prep.**

6. My most vivid memory of my <u>sister</u> is the <u>day</u> she asked <u>me</u> to drink a <u>jar</u> of pickle <u>juice</u>.

Directions: Make up your own complements to fit the spaces provided

                  IO   DO   OP

1. Erin gave _____ a _____ on the _____.

                      DO   OP

2. Erin smacked _____ in the _____.

                              PA

3. The fried cheese tasted _____.

                      OP   PN

4. The little kid in the _____ is _____.

                      IO   DO

5. Adam brought _____ a dead _____.

Directions: Identify the underlined words as direct object, indirect object, object of the preposition, predicate adjective, or predicate nominative.

Remember that if you have an <u>action verb</u>, you are looking for a DO or IO.

If you have a <u>preposition</u>, look for a noun at the end of the prepositional phrase, which will be the OP.

If you have a <u>linking verb</u>, look for a PA or PN.

1. Dudley was <u>furious</u> when the careless driver slid into his new sports car.

2. Chocolate chip and peanut butter brownies are <u>delicious</u> and <u>fattening</u>.

3. Bonzo's strawberry dessert would look and taste <u>better</u> with <u>strawberries</u>.

4. The subjects Bonzo studied were <u>nerdiness</u> and <u>clumsiness</u>.

5. Adam was <u>frustrated</u> with the <u>study</u> of <u>multiplication</u>.

6. That was <u>one</u> of the most embarrassing <u>moments</u> of my <u>life</u>!

7. I was sitting in the <u>movies</u> with a <u>date</u> when I realized I had left a <u>curler</u> in my <u>hair</u>.

8. My parents lectured <u>me</u> about my <u>temper</u>.

9. My parents gave me a lecture on slamming <u>doors</u>, throwing dishes, and kicking holes in the <u>wall</u>.

10. My temper was the <u>worst</u> in the <u>neighborhood</u>.

Exercise F: complements
Directions: Identify the underlined words as subject, PA, PN, DO, IO, OP.

1. <u>Adam</u> is the <u>boy</u> with the overgrown <u>hair</u> and the wild look in his <u>eyes</u>.

2. Adam squished his <u>hand</u> in the door.

3. Adam and Gavin drew <u>pictures</u> of <u>elephants</u> on Trevor's <u>legs</u>.

4. Adam looks silly with his broken <u>glasses</u> and short <u>hair</u>.

5. Gavin gave <u>Trevor</u> the <u>cookie</u> that had fallen on the <u>floor</u>.

6. Adam told <u>Trevor</u> his cereal was crawling with invisible <u>ants</u>.

7. Murphy looked <u>guilty</u>; <u>she</u> had just eaten the <u>last</u> of the pie.

Exercise G: complements
Directions: Identify the underlined words as subject, verb, PA, PN, DO, IO, and OP.

One of my earliest memories of my little <u>brother is</u> the <u>day</u> he smashed <u>me</u> over the <u>head</u> with a <u>brick</u>. <u>I</u> was <u>five</u>; he was three. From the time he was in <u>diapers</u> until he graduated from high school, Charles drove <u>me</u> crazy. Although he looked a little goofy, <u>Charles</u> was <u>clever</u> and <u>sneaky</u>. He knew how to torture <u>me</u>, particularly during my teenage years. He hid behind the <u>couch</u> where I sat with my boyfriend and took notes on our conversations.

Complements
Directions: Identify the underlined as DO, IO, OP, PA, or PN:

1. During one of my temper <u>tantrums</u>, I kicked a <u>hole</u> in the kitchen <u>wall</u>.

2. Frances and I told <u>Adam</u> a <u>story</u> about a magical chocolate <u>chip</u> that loved little boys.

3. My friend sold my <u>sister</u> and <u>me</u> a 1957 red <u>Chevy</u>.

4. After I gobbled three <u>hamburgers</u> and two <u>bags</u> of french <u>fries</u>, I felt <u>awful</u>.

5. Adam's model of <u>China</u> looks a little <u>small</u>.

6. Adam squashed his <u>model</u> of <u>China</u>.

7. The boys in the <u>corner</u> are <u>Hans</u> and <u>David</u>.

8. Adam looks <u>goofy</u> in his purple <u>shirt</u> and orange <u>tie</u>.

9. My friend gave <u>me</u> a concert <u>shirt</u>.

10. Bonzo is the <u>boy</u> who seems to get into trouble constantly.

11. Some children are <u>bored</u> and <u>cranky</u>, but you are not.

12. Adam's plan was to squish his uneaten <u>carrots</u> inside the empty milk <u>carton</u>.

13. Noah and Tim are excellent <u>helpers</u> when I need work done quickly.

ONE **reason to study complements:** to help correct errors with personal pronouns

Example:

1. Me and my friend Bonzo are the clowns of the class.
2. My mom gave my brother and I a lecture about fighting.
3. The books belong to Dan and I.

Sound right? Well, they're wrong. Why?

Only these pronouns can be used as subjects or PNs:

I

he

she

we

they

Only these pronouns can be used as objects (DO, IO, OP):

me

him

her

us

them

Example:

subject   **verb**

1. _____ and my friend Bonzo are the clowns of the class.

Which pronoun should be used as a subject, "I" or "me"?

2. My friend Bonzo and I are the clowns of the class.

Personal Pronouns

Example:

1. My mom gave my brother and _____ a lecture about fighting.

 gave what?   lecture = DO
 to whom?   = IO

Which pronoun should be used as an IO, "I" or "me"?

My mom gave my brother and <u>me</u> a lecture about fighting.

Example:

1. The books belong to Dan and _____.

      to = preposition

 to whom = object of preposition

Which pronoun should be used as an OP, "I" or "me"?

The books belong to Dan and <u>me</u>.

Note: This problem seems to come up only when kids (or adults, for that matter) are talking or writing about <u>two</u> or more people. For example, no one says:

 "My mom gave I a lecture."
 "Me is the clown of the class."
 "The book belongs to I."

If you forget the rules for personal pronouns, you can still avoid making mistakes by thinking about how the sentence would sound if only <u>one</u> person were involved.

Example:

1. My sister called my brother and ____I, me____ last night.
   My sister called "I" or my sister called "me"?
   My sister called <u>me</u> last night.

Exercise H: use of personal pronouns
Directions: 1) Correct the use of the pronouns in the following sentences, if necessary.
2) If the pronoun is correct, explain why.
3) If the pronoun is incorrect, explain why.

Example:

me   OP
Please make sure the films are given to Betsy and I.

OK   PN
"This is he," answered Trevor when I asked for him during the telephone conversation.

"It's me" is widely accepted as a correct response on the telephone, but to be proper, answer "It is I" or "This is he," or "This is she"

1. "It's me!" shouted Todd when I asked who was on the telephone.

2. My father loved to lecture my sister and me about safe driving, staying up past midnight, and going out with long-haired boys.

3. D.T., Diane, and me created a delicious dessert made with whipped cream, honey, and walnuts.

4. My sister Frances says my brother and me have trouble following directions.

5. She often laughs and claims the only solution is to build Play-Dough models of her directions for my brother and I.

Correct Use of Personal Pronouns

Directions: Decide which personal pronoun should be used and circle your answer.

1. The secret of the missing cookies is between Adam and (I, me).

2. (She, Her), Bonzo, and Fred dyed their hair orange.

3. (Me, I) and Dudley have baked an elegant dessert for Tim, John, and (he, him).

4. The keys to the sports car belong to Tim, Adam, and (I, me).

5. "This is (him, he)," answered Dudley when Suzanne asked for (he, him) on the telephone.

6. Emilie says Dudley and (I, me) make very fattening brownies.

7. Give that list of wild, disobedient kids to (me, I) and the principal.

8. Using an electric razor, Bill gave Brendan and (he, him) a disastrous buzz-saw haircut.

9. It is important that Sean, Sam, and (she, her) make many desserts for the student party.

10. Digby and (me, I) chased the mouse around the house.

11. The books under the bed belong to Adam and (I, me).

12. My father gave Ann and (I, me) a long lecture on safe driving.

13. The teacher said Connie and (I, me) would be punished for writing notes in class.

PHRASES

1. Prepositional phrases

2. Verb phrases

   a. participial phrase

   b. gerund phrase

   c. infinitive phrase

3. Appositive phrases

Phrases

A Phrase:

1) is a group of words that belongs together
2) does not have a subject
3) is used as a single part of speech

There Are Three Kinds of Phrases:

1) prepositional phrases
2) verb phrases
   a. participial
   b. gerund
   c. infinitive
3) appositive phrases

You can learn to identify a phrase by studying what makes a prepositional phrase.

Example: on the table
in the refrigerator
on Murphy's head

You can see that there's no subject or complete thought in any of these phrases.

Examples of Other Kinds of Phrases:

dressed in a ridiculous outfit
whispering in study hall
by tying the sheets together

Prepositional Phrases

Prepositions:

1)   almost always show position

2)   always come in phrases

           and

3)   prepositional phrases are used as adjectives and called adjective phrases

           or

4)   prepositional phrases are used as adverbs and called adverb phrases

Prepositional Phrases = Adjective Phrase or Adverb Phrase

How can you tell the difference between a prepositional phrase that is an adjective and one that is an adverb?

Adjective Phrases do what adjectives do: they describe Nouns

Example:

noun

The vampire at your doorstep is Dracula.

    Which vampire?

    the one at your doorstep

at your doorstep is a prep. phrase describing a noun

What is the only part of speech that can describe a noun?

    An adjective.

    at your doorstep is an adjective phrase

noun⤺ | **adj. phrase** |

The vampire | at your doorstep | is Dracula.

Another example of an adjective phrase:

noun

The black cat with the vampire fangs is Murphicula.

     Which cat?

     the one with the vampire fangs

with the vampire fangs is a prep. phrase describing the noun, cat

What is the only part of speech that describes a noun?

     An adjective.

with the vampire fangs is an adjective phrase

noun

The black cat | **adj. phrase** with the vampire fangs | is Murphicula.

Adverb Phrases do what adverbs do: they Describe **1) Verbs**

                                     2) Adjectives

                                     3) Other Adverbs

AND answer the questions:

     1) WHEN?

     2) WHERE?

     3) WHY?

     4) HOW?

     5) HOW LONG?

     6) HOW MUCH?

Adverb Phrases

Example: The desperate vampire lunged **v.** | **adv. phrase** for his coffin.

Lunged where?

for his coffin

lunged is a verb

for his coffin tells where he lunged

What is the only part of speech that can describe a verb?

An adverb.

for his coffin is an adverb phrase

Example: Bonzo looked ridiculous **adj.** | **adv. phrase** in his frog outfit.

ridiculous is an adjective describing the noun Bonzo

ridiculous in what?

in his frog outfit

in his frog outfit is describing the adjective ridiculous

What is the only part of speech that describes an adjective?

An adverb.

in his frog outfit is an adverb phrase

Example: School starts later **v.** **adv.** | **adv. phrase** in September than I thought.

Starts when?

later

later is an adverb describing the verb starts

Later when?

in September

in September tells how much later;
it describes later

What is the only part of speech that describes an adverb?

Another adverb.

in September is an adverb phrase

Adjective and Adverb Phrases

More Samples:

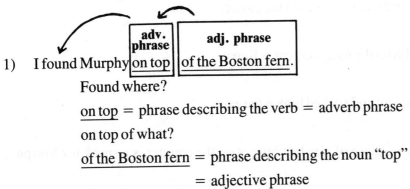

1)   I found Murphy on top of the Boston fern.

Found where?

on top = phrase describing the verb = adverb phrase

on top of what?

of the Boston fern = phrase describing the noun "top"

= adjective phrase

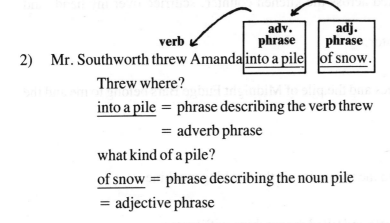

2)   Mr. Southworth threw Amanda into a pile of snow.

Threw where?

into a pile = phrase describing the verb threw

= adverb phrase

what kind of a pile?

of snow = phrase describing the noun pile

= adjective phrase

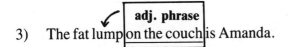

3)   The fat lump on the couch is Amanda.

Which lump?

on the couch = phrase describing the noun lump

= adjective phrase

Prepositional Phrases as Adjective and Adverb Phrases

Directions: 1) Place the prepositional phrases in parentheses.
2) Identify the prepositional phrase as an <u>adjective</u> or <u>adverb</u> phrase.

1.   I hid the dirty clothes behind my shoes in the closet.

2.   The skinny, ugly kid with the nasty haircut is Bonzo.

3.   Lilly bit Adam on the arm and socked him in the eye.

4.   The squishy, disgusting piece of raw hamburger on the counter is a snack for Murphy.

5.   The cats in the house pay no attention to the presence of mice.

6.   The chubby mouse streaked across the kitchen counter, scurried over my hand, and leaped behind the refrigerator.

7.   The box of Krazy Krunchies and the pile of Midnight Fudge Bars belong to me and the mice.

8.   Mr. Southworth discovered the mouse inside the washing machine.

9.   He chose the "spin-dry" cycle and filled the machine with water.

10. The mouse leaped from the washing machine, scurried past Mr. Southworth, and ran toward safety.

Exercise A

Directions: 1) Circle the prepositional phrases.
2) Draw an arrow to the word they describe.
3) Label as either adjective or adverb phrase.

Example:

adv. phrase

The spaghetti sauce is simmering (in the pot.)

1. Midnight Fudge Bars melt in your mouth.

2. The gooey dessert is covered with caramels and butterscotch.

3. Peter sank his teeth into the giant fudge cookie.

4. Adam jumped into the closet.

5. Amanda snarled and smacked Adam on the head.

6. Frankenstein was created in a small, desolate village in Transylvania.

7. The vampire with the long, sharp bloody teeth hypnotized me with his red eyes.

8. Werewolves rarely sleep during a full moon; they are too busy looking for a tasty meal.

9. Last Halloween Trevor was Dracula; he waxed his hair with grease, covered his

   face with white make-up, and smeared fake blood on his fangs.

Prepositional Phrases

Directions: 1) Locate the prepositional phrases and place them in parentheses.
2) Identify the prepositional phrase as an <u>Adjective</u> or <u>Adverb</u> phrase.

1. The handsome boy with the blue eyes is Gavin.

2. Suddenly a mouse streaked across the living room.

3. The lump under the chair is Amanda.

4. The gerbils slid down the plastic tubes on their backs.

5. Lamar, the fattest gerbil, was eating a pile of newspapers.

6. The mouse sat on the kitchen table and stared at me.

7. My brother created stories about monsters for Adam.

8. The ball bounced off my head and landed on the floor.

9. Adam danced to his favorite songs on the radio.

10. We raced for the van.

11. The van in the parking lot is ours.

12. Adam wore his fluorescent orange tie to school.

13. Adam threw his arms around my neck in an attempt to give me "the cobra clutch."

14. Murphy slept by the side of the bed.

15. Murphy slept by the mice nest.

Comma Rule for Prepositional Phrases:

If a sentence <u>begins</u> with <u>2</u> or more prepositional phrases, put a comma at the end of the last phrase.

Example: In the middle of the night, I heard a faint scratching at my window.

                         phrases: in the middle

                         of the night

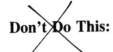

Don't Do This:

Wrong: In the middle, of the night, I heard a faint scratching at my window.

OR

Wrong: I heard a faint scratching at my window in the middle, of the night.

Exercise B

Directions: Make comma corrections <u>if</u> necessary.

1. Through the opening, in the curtain, I saw a shadow outside my window.

2. I knew a stranger was waiting for me, outside the window.

3. I trembled, with fear.

4. Outside the window on the screen, a long, thin, white hand pressed on the glass.

5. I edged closer to the window, for a better look.

6. Behind the door in his room, Ajax waited, impatiently.

7. Ajax waited with impatience, behind the door in his room.

8. After the end of a long wait it was time for Ajax to sneak out of the house.

9. His eyes glowed in the dark, in the still room.

10. Behind the tree in the front yard his best friend waited with a pile of water balloons.

11. Ajax crept noiselessly across his room, in his bare feet.

12. He slid the window open, with great skill and care and disappeared into the night.

Using Prepositional Phrases for Sentence Variety:

Begin sentences with prepositional phrases to add variety and break monotony in your writing.

Example: Bonzo waited on her doorstep with flowers in one hand and a can of soda in the other.

With flowers in one hand and a can of soda in the other, Bonzo waited on her doorstep.

There is a dark, deserted house on the other side of the forest.

On the other side of the forest, there is a dark, deserted house.

Old coins are said to be buried in the cellar of the house.

In the cellar of the house, old coins are said to be buried.

Using Prepositional Phrases for Sentence Variety

Directions: Practice making sentences more varied by using introductory prepositional phrases in the following sentences:

1. The ghost passed silently through the door in the hallway.

2. The ghost beckoned to me from the top of the stairs.

3. Three whispy ghosts flew above my head.

4. The smiling ghost leaned against the doorway to my room.

5. A charming yellow scarf dangled from the transparent neck of the ghost.

6. I could see the chic ghost in his tuxedo beside the lawn chairs on the patio.

7. The ghost's drink rested on a wicker table in the backyard.

8. Pearl buttons glimmered on the front of the ghost's snow white shirt.

9. The ghost whispered my name in a soft, fragile voice.

10. I decided to join him on the spur of the moment.

Verb Phrases

There Are Three Kinds of Verb Phrases:

1) participial
2) gerund
3) infinitive

Participial Phrases

Participals:
Participial Phrases:

1) usually end in "ing" or "ed"
2) are called verb phrases because there is action in the phrase
3) always work as adjectives because they describe nouns

A <u>verb</u> phrase that is an <u>adjective</u>?

Classified as a phrase, participial phrases are verb phrases.

Classified as a part of speech, participial phrases work as adjectives.

They involve <u>action</u>, but they <u>describe a noun</u>.

PARTICIPIAL

Example: noun
Adam, confused by my sudden decision, fainted.

Where's the action?

being confused

Who is confused?

Adam = noun

PARTICIPIAL PHRASE

participial phrase   noun
Sneaking through the dark halls, Amanda discovered the thawing chicken and devoured the entire package.

Where's the action?

sneaking

Who is sneaking?

Amanda = noun

Exercise C
Directions: 1) Underline the participial phrase.
2) Draw an arrow to the noun it describes.

1. The burly weight lifter, renowned for power lifting, hefted the barbells and grunted furiously.

2. Heaving with all her might, the lifter slammed the weights together with a tremendous shove.

3. Groaning with effort, Ajax heaved eighty ten-pound plates.

4. Susan spent much of her time dodging Bonzo in the hallways.

5. Smiling politely, Mr. Southworth asked Amanda if she wanted a free trip to the moon.

Comma Rule for Participial Phrases:

Use a comma after a participial phrase that <u>begins</u> a sentence.

Example: Exhausted by his captivity in the toy box, Trevor collapsed.

Exercise D
Directions: 1) Use these participial phrases in a sentence.
2) Make sure they describe a noun.
3) Set off the participial phrase with a comma when necessary.

1. defeated by her refusal to go out with him

2. laughing hysterically

3. feeling ridiculous

4. embarrassed by his new haircut

5. outraged by her decision

6. approaching her cautiously

7. sleeping calmly at his desk

8. loaded with hilarious stories

9. snoring peacefully

10. worked into a frenzy

11. attracted to the tray of pastries

12. flopping into the classroom desk

13. tired of Bonzo's love letters

14. kicking the wall in frustration

15. working feverishly to finish his biology project

Participial Phrases

Directions: 1) The participal is underlined.
　　　　　　　 2) Place the participial phrase in parentheses.
　　　　　　　 3) Draw an arrow to the noun it describes.

1.   <u>Stunned</u> by the blow to his ego, Ajax fell to the ground.

2.   <u>Embarrassed</u> by the love notes, Bonzo blushed.

3.   Mr. Doolittle, <u>renowned</u> for his difficult algebra tests, often made life a little unpleasant.

4.   My mother, <u>annoyed</u> with my constant crankiness, banished me to my room for the remainder of the evening.

5.   <u>Slithering</u> through the halls, the snake looked for prey.

6.   <u>Leaping</u> over the couch, Murphy made a dash for the mouse.

7.   <u>Moving</u> quickly, Murphy grabbed the mouse.

Participial Phrases

Directions: 1) Underline the participal.
2) Circle the participial phrase.
3) Draw an arrow to the noun it describes.

1. Dressed in their Halloween costumes, the kids ran off to "trick or treat."

2. Seeking the ugliest monster mask he could find, Adam toured the aisles of the dime store.

3. Adam, disguised as a Martian, rang all the doorbells in the neighborhood.

4. On Halloween night I stood at the door armed with caramel apples and Midnight Fudge Bars.

5. Struggling inside his gorilla costume, Bonzo cried sorrowfully.

6. Trevor, angered with his rather small collection of candy, crushed his pumpkin costume in frustration.

7. Running wildly in fright, Adam escaped from the boy in the Dracula costume.

8. Having completed his trick or treating, Adam returned home.

9. Grinning at the thought of his stuffed Halloween bag, Adam drifted off to sleep.

10. Adam handed me the gift tied with blue ribbon.

11. Amanda padding down the hall made an eerie sound.

12. Terrified of being tossed outside, Murphy hid from Mr. Southworth.

Using Participial Phrases in Your Writing

Combine ho-hum, short sentences by using participial phrases.

Example: Bonzo climbed out of the window of the science lab. We saw him.

We saw Bonzo climbing out of the window of the science lab.

Example: Adam burned his hand on the coils.

He stood too close to the stove.

Standing too close to the stove, Adam burned his hand on the coils.

Exercise E
Directions: Combine each of the following groups of sentences into one sentence by using a participial phrase.

1. Ajax was delighted with my invitation to a shrimp dinner.
    He accepted immediately.

    _____

    _____

    _____

2. The schoolbus screamed down the hill.
    It barely missed the group of joggers on the road.

    _____

    _____

    _____

3. Adam escaped from the little girl.
    He blushed furiously until she released him.

    _____

    _____

    _____

Verb Phrases:

WORK AS ADJECTIVES	WORK AS NOUNS	WORK AS ADVERBS, ADJECTIVES OR NOUNS
◆	◆	◆
1) Participial	2) Gerund	3) Infinitive

Gerunds and Gerund Phrases = NOUNS

Gerunds:	1) usually end in "ing"
Gerund Phrases:	2) are called verb phrases because there is action in the phrase
	3) always work as a noun

A <u>verb</u> phrase that is a <u>noun</u>?
Classified as a phrase, gerund phrases are verb phrases.

Classified as a part of speech, gerund phrases work as nouns.

They involve <u>action</u>, but they work as <u>nouns</u>.

So, <u>as nouns</u>, gerunds or gerund phrases will be a subject, a direct object, the object of the preposition, or a predicate nominative.

Example:

     gerund   **gerund phrase**
    Running several miles a day involves more exercise than walking.

What involves more exercise?

running several miles a day

running several miles a day is the subject of the verb involves

   <u>running several miles a day</u> = gerund phrase

Where is the action?

running is the action

Why is it a noun?

It is the subject of the sentence.

Example:

> I enjoy lifting weights.
>
> What is the action?
>
> lifting
>
> lifting weights = verb phrase
>
> Enjoy what?
>
> lifting weights
>
> <u>lifting weights</u> = direct object
>
> action = direct object = gerund phrase

Example:

> I avoid "flabitis" by lifting weights.
>
> What is the action?
>
> lifting
>
> lifting weights = verb phrase
>
> By what?
>
> by lifting weights
>
> <u>lifting weights</u> = object of prep. "by"
>
> action = object of prep. = gerund phrase

Gerund Phrases

Exercise F
Directions: 1) The gerund has been underlined.
2) Underline the gerund phrase and explain how it is used as a noun: subject? PN? DO? or OP?

1. For <u>toning</u> muscles and building strength, lift weights.

2. <u>Losing</u> fifty pounds improved her appearance.

3. <u>Imitating</u> frogs and faculty members is Bonzo's claim to fame.

4. <u>Creating</u> new Dracula stories for Adam is entertaining and fun.

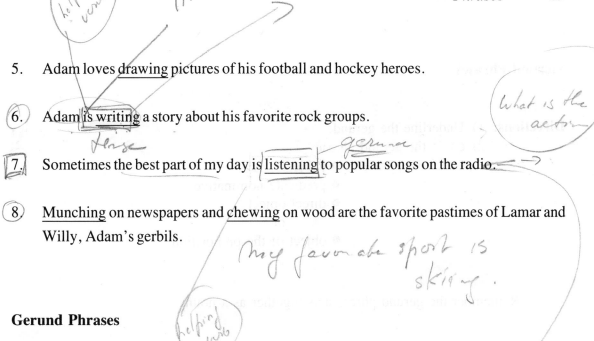

5. Adam loves drawing pictures of his football and hockey heroes.

6. Adam is writing a story about his favorite rock groups.

7. Sometimes the best part of my day is listening to popular songs on the radio.

8. Munching on newspapers and chewing on wood are the favorite pastimes of Lamar and Willy, Adam's gerbils.

Gerund Phrases

Directions: Underline the gerund phrases in the following sentences:

1. Driving in traffic is often the worst part of commuting.

2. Adam's favorite pastime is playing hockey.

3. I enjoy telling Adam ghost stories.

4. Mr. Doolittle made his point by storming out of the room.

5. Eating three pies a day is a sure way to gain weight.

Gerund Phrases

Directions: 1) Underline the gerund.
2) circle the gerund phrase.
3) Label the phrase as ● subject
● predicate nominative
● direct object
or
● object of the preposition

Remember the gerund phrase acts together as a noun.

1. Walking on his hands was one of Bonzo's stupid attention-getting methods.

2. Bonzo loves dissecting frogs and toads.

3. Telling the difference between the gorilla and Bonzo is a challenge.

4. Bonzo hated the chore of removing his gorilla costume.

5. An entertaining spectacle is watching Bonzo struggle with his gorilla costume.

6. Bonzo's favorite activity is chasing little kids with frogs.

7. Bonzo debated about eating the raw frog.

8. Cooking frog legs the correct way is difficult and challenging.

9. Bonzo enjoys creating interesting meals.

10. He discussed the merits of baking the frog legs in a garlic sauce.

Verb Phrases:

1) Participial   2) Gerund   3) Infinitive

Infinitives and Infinitive Phrases

<u>Infinitives:</u>   1) are verbs usually beginning with "to"

<u>Infinitive Phrases:</u>   2) begin with the word "to"

3) can be used as a — noun

— adjective

<u>or</u>

— adverb

<u>Infinitive phrases</u> are the easiest of all! Just look for the word "to," check to see if it is followed by a verb, and presto, you have an <u>infinitive</u>. Then, look for all the words that seem to fit with the infinitive, and you have an <u>infinitive phrase</u>.

Example: To plan an elegant seafood dinner is my project today.

infinitive: to plan

infinitive phrase: to plan an elegant seafood dinner

Example: Bonzo is the person to see about the hole in the wall.

infinitive: to see

infinitive phrase: to see about the hole

Some infinitives do not begin with "to," but most of them do. Because the word "to" is such a helpful clue in finding infinitives, it's not really necessary to be able to tell <u>how</u> the infinitive phrase is used in the sentence in order to identify it.

Infinitive phrases are used as nouns, adjectives, or adverbs, but for practical purposes, all you really need to do is look for the phrase itself.

Exercise G
Directions: Underline the infinitive phrases.

1. We had hoped to sneak out the back door.

2. To take karate lessons is Adam's dream.

3. Adam and Gavin were glad to escape from the older boys.

4. To break out of the fort, Adam and Gavin pushed with all their might against the wooden door.

5. Everyone found it easy to laugh at Bonzo.

Infinitive Phrases

Directions: 1) Underline the infinitive.
              2) Circle the infinitive phrase.

1. The trick to good soups is to stir them frequently as they cook.

2. To learn the skill of pie making is difficult.

3. To make Hunan crispy beef properly is hard.

4. Adam wants to be the chef this evening.

5. To eat what he has cooked is his greatest challenge.

6. Adam forgot to stir the pudding.

7. Chris and Steve planned to create a delicious ice cream pie.

8. David and Matthew have learned to use cheese in many delicious sauces.

9. To charm as many girls as possible is Teddy's goal in life.

10. Gavin added softened butter to his bread recipe to make the dough a little easier to knead.

Infinitive Phrases

Directions: Identify the infinitive phrases in the following sentences:

1. To plan a party is sometimes fun.

2. Adam is the person to see about the missing gerbils.

3. We hoped to leave at noon, but Adam couldn't find Lamar and Willy, his gerbils.

4. To forget embarrassing high school experiences is one of my goals in life.

5. Adam offered to find Lamar and Willy.

6. To be a professional hockey player is Adam's dream.

7. We hoped to sneak into the cafeteria.

8. Adam wanted desperately to win his first hockey game.

9. It is often difficult to open peanut butter jars.

10. Adam began to sob when he discovered the cats sleeping on his plastic model of China.

Exercise H

Directions: 1) Underline the phrases in the following sentences.
         2) Label each phrase as either <u>prepositional phrase</u>, <u>participial phrase</u>, <u>gerund phrase</u>, or <u>infinitive phrase</u>.

1. Annoyed by his constant chattering in class, Mr. Doolittle took out a pair of scissors and cut off Timothy's tie.

2. Murphy has learned to open doors with her paws.

3. Slamming his fist against the wall, Bonzo screamed in frustration and anger.

4. My dream is to build a house in the mountains of Colorado.

5. Ajax was punished for placing the dead rat in Robert's classroom desk.

Exercise I

Directions: Write <u>3</u> sentences that <u>begin</u> with prepositional phrases; be sure to use commas correctly.

_____

_____

_____

_____

Exercise J

Directions: Write <u>3</u> sentences that <u>begin</u> with participial phrases; be sure to use commas correctly.

_____

_____

_____

_____

Exercise K

Directions: Write <u>3</u> sentences that <u>begin</u> with infinitive phrases.

_____

_____

_____

_____

Exercise L

Directions: Answer the following questions or explain:

1. Both participial phrases and gerund phrases can begin with words ending in "ing." How do you tell the difference between the two?

2. When is the word "to" part of an infinitive phrase and when is it a preposition?

3. How can gerund phrases be verbs and nouns at the same time?

4. How can participial phrases be verbs and adjectives at the same time?

5. What do the comma rules for phrases have in common?

Appositive Phrases

The word "appositive" gets its meaning from a Latin word meaning "to place side by side."

Appositive phrases and the noun or pronoun they explain are placed side by side.

Appositive phrase: 1) is a group of words that explains who or what the noun is
                      2) is before or right after the noun it explains

Example:

1. Adam, <u>my nine year old son</u>, is a fanatic Bruins' fan.

    Who is Adam?

    my nine year old son

    <u>my nine year old son</u> = appositive phrase

2. Dudley, <u>Bonzo's best friend</u>, usually gets into unbelievable trouble when his parents go out of town.

    Who is Dudley?

    Bonzo's best friend = appositive phrase describing the noun, Dudley

3. Amanda, <u>the champion cat complainer</u>, begged for a treat, <u>a peanut butter and jelly sandwich</u>.

    Who is Amanda?

    <u>the champion cat complainer</u> = appositive phrase

    What treat?

    <u>a peanut butter and jelly sandwich</u> = appositive phrase

Appositive Phrases

Directions: 1. Underline the appositive phrase in each sentence.
2. Draw an arrow to the noun or pronoun it explains.

1. George, one of my favorite students, enjoys hiding my coffee cups.

2. My classroom, the room at the end of the hall, is littered with books, magazines, papers, and plants.

3. Two students of mine, Greg and Max, have been punished for dropping water balloons on the teacher's head.

4. I love my third period class, a collection of comics and entertainers.

5. Billy Hall, a most intriguing student, has perfected the art of walking backwards.

Directions: 1. Using the following phrases as guides, create five sentences with appositive phrases.
2. Underline the appositive phrase and draw an arrow to the noun or pronoun it explains.

1. the meanest kid on the block

2. Dudley and Bonzo

3. Bavarian apple torte

4. the boy with the orange hair

5. An avid detective story fan

Appositive Phrases

Directions: Identify the appositive phrases in the following sentences.

1. My old math teacher, Mr. Doolittle, once stood on his desk and threw chalk out the window.

2. The advisor for the school yearbook, I am often busy taking photographs and creating layouts.

3. Adam and his friends have a new club, the "Insiders."

4. Biology tests are usually on Friday, the worst day of the week.

5. Oscar, the largest cat I ever owned, weighed almost thirty pounds.

6. A boy of extreme clumsiness, Bonzo bounced across the dance floor.

7. Adam, the boy with the spaghetti sauce on his chin, is my son.

8. The boy with the spaghetti sauce on his chin, Adam, is my son.

Exercise M
Directions: Underline each appositive phrase and draw an arrow to the noun or pronoun it explains.

1. Chocolate mousse, an elegant dessert, is made with chocolate, egg whites, and cream.

2. A delicious appetizer, cheese and crab spread, can be made in a few minutes for unexpected company.

3. A man of many words, Bonzo won the speech contest with his talk on frogs.

4. Ajax, the boy wearing the torn-up concert shirt, has several girlfriends.

5. The headmaster of the school, Mr. Doolittle, is always dressed in baggy clothes.

Comma Rules for Appositive Phrases

Appositives and appositive phrases are usually set off by commas.

Example: Everyone, even his mother, thinks Bonzo is a little goofy.

Exercise N
Directions: Place commas when necessary.

1. An amateur photographer I enjoy taking pictures of children.

2. Frogs a major concern of Bonzo's was the topic of his oral presentation.

3. Dog and monkey meat considered a delicacy in the Far East is rejected as food in our country.

4. Adam and Gavin great fans of rock music spend hours listening to the radio.

5. A handsome, charming boy Max has a unique sense of humor.

6. Max a handsome charming boy has a unique sense of humor.

7. My classroom the one with the chewed up rug is located on the second floor of this building.

8. The rug the red one in the middle of the room is a reminder that the cats were too lazy and fat to catch mice.

9. This rug the one stored in the basement throughout the summer became a home for several mice living in our house.

10. Conscientious nest builders the mice chewed off a corner of the rug to make their home more cozy.

Directions: Use the following phrases as appositive phrases in sentences of your own creation. Make sure the phrases are punctuated correctly.

1.   the two lazy cats

_____

_____

_____

2.   the mice sleeping inside the rug

_____

_____

_____

3.   a cat with few brain cells

_____

_____

_____

4.   a meal of stolen cat crunchies

_____

_____

_____

5.   Amanda and Murphy

_____

_____

_____

Using Appositive Phrases in Your Writing

Combine short, choppy sentences using appositive phrases.

Example: Weight lifting is a very popular exercise. It is gaining more fans.
Weight lifting, a most strenuous sport, is gaining more fans.

Exercise O
Directions: Combine each group of sentences by using an appositive phrase; be sure to place commas in the right place.

1. Amanda is the greediest cat I know.
   She races to the food bowl several times a day.

   _____

   _____

   _____

2. Adam is very careless with his clothes.
   He ripped his pants and broke down the backs of his shoes.

   _____

   _____

   _____

3. Bonzo is one of the clumsiest boys in school. He is well known for his free-fall flights down the stairs.

   _____

   _____

   _____

Phrases

Directions: Identify the underlined phrases as   1) prepositional
2) participial
3) gerund
4) infinitive
5) appositive

1. <u>Practicing dance steps</u> requires a good deal of Adam's time.

2. <u>By listening carefully to radio tunes</u>, Adam memorizes the words to dozens of songs.

3. <u>Watching dancers on television</u> inspires Adam to new dancing feats.

4. Adam loves <u>to dance on his bed</u>.

5. <u>After a few crashes to the floor</u>, I convinced Adam to stop dancing on the bed.

6. Leigh, <u>a good friend of Adam's</u>, tried to teach Adam a few tricky maneuvers.

7. <u>Dressed in sequined shirts and green pants</u>, Adam and Leigh danced wildly on the kitchen counters.

8. <u>After their strenuous exercise</u>, both boys collapsed in a heap <u>on the floor</u>.

CLAUSES

1. Independent clauses

2. Subordinate clauses

   a. adjective clauses

   b. adverb clauses

   c. noun clauses

Clauses

A Clause: 1) is a group of words used as part of a sentence

2) has a subject and a verb

There are 2 kinds of CLAUSES:

1) independent clauses
2) subordinate clauses

Independent Clauses

Independent clauses are called "independent" because they can stand alone as sentences. They have the three essential parts to a sentence: a subject, a verb, and a complete thought.

Independent clauses are really sentences. They are called clauses when they are hooked to another clause.

Example:

1. Adam became very sick. = sentence

   After he devoured seven Midnight Fudge Bars, Adam became very sick.

   Adam became very sick = now a clause because it's linked to another part of the sentence.

2. The cats had turned the living room into a race track. = sentence

   The cats had turned the living room into a race track, and pillows, lamps, cushions, and books had toppled to the floor.

   The cats had turned the living room into a race track = independent clause because it's connected with another part of the sentence.

Independent clauses can be joined with <u>a comma and a conjunction</u>, or they can be joined with a <u>semi-colon</u>.

➔ see p. 21

Example:

1. I heard a rustling in the large garbage can, and I peered over the edge.

    <u>first independent clause</u>: I heard a rustling in the garbage can

    <u>second independent clause</u>: I peered over the edge

    <u>joined by</u>: , and   *nor*
    but   *for*
    or   *yet*

2. A fat furry face popped out of the crumpled papers, empty pizza boxes, and old milk cartons; it was Murphy.

    <u>first independent clause</u>: A fat furry face popped out of the crumpled papers, empty pizza boxes, and old milk cartons

    <u>second independent clause</u>: it was Murphy

    <u>joined by</u>: ;

3. Murphy was scavenging for snacks, and she wasn't too pleased about being interrupted.

    What are the two independent clauses?

    What joins the clauses?

Subordinate Clauses *are fragments!*

"Subordinate" comes from the Latin prefix, "sub," meaning beneath or below. For our purposes, "subordinate" means ranked below. Subordinate clauses are "below" independent clauses because they cannot stand by themselves.

A Subordinate Clause:

1) has a subject and a verb

2) does not have a complete thought

3) cannot stand by itself

4) needs an independent clause to complete its meaning

independent clause = sentence
subordinate clause = fragment

Subordinate clauses are sometimes called **DEPENDENT CLAUSES** because they depend on the rest of the sentence to make it a whole

Example:

- because she had spent the morning in the garbage bins
- after she had her fill of old pizza crusts
- for which she had been searching

1. Because she had spent the morning in the garbage bins, Murphy was filthy.
    subordinate clause: because she had spent the morning in the garbage bins
    independent clause: Murphy was filthy

2. Murphy struggled out of the bin after she had her fill of old pizza crusts.
    subordinate clause: after she had her fill of old pizza crusts
    independent clause: Murphy struggled out of the bin

3. She found the snack for which she had been searching.
    subordinate clause: for which she had been searching
    independent clause: she found the snack

Exercise A
Directions: Find and label independent and subordinate clauses.

Example:
                                    ind. clause
        There were no actresses in Shakespeare's time;

               ind. clause
        men played all the female roles.

            ind. clause   sub. clause
        Everyone cheered until Mr. Doolittle asked for silence.

1.   Everyone cheered; school was cancelled.

2.   When Adam and Gavin bounced on the top bunk, it crashed to the floor.

3.   Ajax hurled the grammar book in frustration, and he stormed from the room.

4.   The grammar book sailed across the schoolroom, and it smacked into the wall behind the teacher on duty.

5.   The students in the study hall waited nervously; would the teacher fling the book back at them?

6.   The teacher calmly retrieved the book from the floor, and business went on as usual.

Finding Subordinate and Independent Clauses

Directions: Find and label any independent or subordinate clauses.

1. Adam hid in the closet, and he waited for his parents to leave the house.

2. When I visited my sister in New York City last summer, we toured all the interesting shops in the Village.

3. Gag gifts that Frances loves to buy for practical jokes were on display in several shops.

4. There were pink plastic flamingos, plastic noses, and fright wigs on display; we also saw hand buzzers and wild hats.

5. Adam enjoys Frances's gifts because he loves hand buzzers, vampire pens, and plastic snakes.

Subordinate Clauses

There are 3 kinds of subordinate clauses:
1) adjective clauses
2) adverb clauses
3) noun clauses

Adjective Clauses

Adjective clauses do what adjectives do:

they describe nouns

Example: The bin behind the dorm is the place that Murphy likes the best.

adjective clause: that Murphy likes the best.

Adjective clauses usually begin with:

1) who
2) whom
3) whose
4) which
5) that

These are Called Relative Pronouns

Adverb Clauses

<u>Adverb clauses</u> do what adverbs do:

they describe 1) verbs
2) adjectives
3) other adverbs

Example: After Murphy nibbled on the mouse, she squished it with her paw.

when?

adverb clause: after Murphy nibbled on the mouse

she squished when?

after Murphy nibbled on the mouse = adverb clause telling when and modifying the verb "squished"

<u>Adverb clauses</u> usually begin with subordinating conjunction:

after	before	so that	when
although	if	than	whenever
as	in order that	though	where
because	since	unless	wherever
		until	while

Noun Clauses act as nouns:

They can be
1) subjects
2) predicate nominatives
3) direct objects
4) indirect objects
5) objects of the prepositions

Noun Clauses usually begin with:

1) that
2) what
3) whatever
4) who
5) whoever
6) whom
7) whomever

Example:

1. No one could tell <u>what she had screamed</u>.

> could tell what?
>
> what she had screamed = direct object = noun clause

2. <u>What she screamed</u> surprised me.

> what surprised?
>
> what she screamed = subject of sentence = noun clause

3. Ajax knows <u>what our dark secret is</u>.

> knows what?
>
> what our secret is = direct object = noun clause

Adjective Clauses

Directions: Identify the adjective clause in each of the following sentences:

1. This gooey mess is the art project that Adam has been creating.

2. Is this the papier mâché model of China that we have been waiting for?

3. Freddy is the student who glued the grammar books together.

4. The mess that is simmering in the pot is the glue necessary for Adam's project.

5. This is the school project that everyone talks about!

Adverb Clauses

Directions: Identify the adverb clauses in the following sentences:

1. If you wish to bore me, start talking about professional wrestling.

2. Sometimes Bonzo acts as if he were five years old!

3. Whenever we picnic by the lake, we bring dill sandwiches and grapes.

4. Adam stirred the dirt in the mixing bowl after he added rocks and sticks.

5. Let's plan this joke so that it will be a complete surprise for Mr. Doolittle.

Noun Clauses

Directions: Identify the noun clauses in the following sentences:

1. Whatever is the current fad is a subject of interest to all adolescents.

2. No one could tell what color his hair was originally.

3. Whoever threw the mashed potatoes at Mr. Doolittle's table is in big trouble!

4. Give the tickets to whomever you feel would enjoy the concert.

5. Kathy knows what irritates her brother.

6. No one could tell what Bonzo had brewed in the science lab.

7. The winner will be whoever keeps quiet for the next thirty minutes!

8. We could not tell who was hiding behind the teacher's door.

9. What I like most about cooking is eating the results.

10. That he had the courage to walk into the class of rowdy students was interesting.

11. Bonzo received a kiss for what he had accomplished.

Exercise B

Directions: 1) Underline each subordinate clause.
                2) Label the subordinate clause as either an adjective clause, an adverb clause, or a noun clause.

1.   Trevor will do whatever Adam and Gavin tell him.

2.   Here is the mouse for which Murphy has been waiting.

3.   Whenever I got the urge, I devoured dozens of ice cream sandwiches.

4.   Before I went to bed at night, I ate several bowls of frozen mixed vegetables smothered in garlic salt.

5.   Midnight is the hour for which Dracula has been longing.

Exercise C

Directions: Answer the following questions:

1.   What is the difference between an independent clause and a subordinate clause?

2.   What is the difference between a subordinate clause and a phrase?

Subordinate Clauses

Directions: Label the underlined subordinate clauses as
1) adjective clause
2) adverb clause
   or
3) noun clause

1. Barry, <u>whose twitching eyebrows expressed his anxieties</u>, was a favorite dog in our house.

2. Barry would do <u>whatever my brother told him</u>.

3. We knew <u>that Barry was extremely jealous of our other pets</u>; he also loved to eat.

4. My sister used to hold up a can of dog food <u>while my brother petted the cat</u>.

5. Barry sat in between the cat and the dog food and whined <u>because he didn't know which to go after first</u>.

6. <u>How the turkey was stolen from the table</u> is another family dog story.

7. <u>Whenever we went out for ice cream</u>, Barry got his own cone.

8. A strawberry cone was <u>what Barry always wanted</u>.

9. Another strange habit <u>that Barry had</u> was sitting in front of the steering wheel of the car; he wanted to drive.

10. <u>Whenever my father told him he couldn't ride in the truck</u>, Barry got sick.

Subordinate Clauses: Adjective, Noun, and Adverb Clauses

Directions: Are the groups of words in the parentheses adjective, noun, or adverb clauses? OR, are they <u>mistakes</u>?

1.   It's amazing how Dudley does his homework in class, but (no matter how I try to attract her attention), the teacher never notices.

2.   (After Mike won his match), he was disappointed to see we lost the meet.

3.   I think (that staying in school over vacation is a dumb idea).

4.   Everyone knew (who climbed on top of the roof).

5.   (Whoever went with John) is lucky.

6.   (Until tomorrow) there won't be a way for us to get together.

7.   You are going (to be great someday).

8.   No one could guess (what the answer was).

9.   I was bored with the program (until Dracula appeared on stage).

10.   Barry, (my overweight dog), picked on our neighbor's cat (who was a chump).

11.   The orange juice (that tasted sour) was thrown out.

12.   The excited Murphy jumped on the table and devoured the crispy apricot cake, (which took hours to make).

Comma Rules for Clauses

1.   <u>Use a comma before</u>:   and

but

or

nor

for

<u>and</u>   yet

when they join independent clauses.

Example:

1.   I made a lemon cream pie, BUT I forgot the butter.

2.   First Adam dropped the eggs on the floor, AND he stepped in the yellow mess.

NOTE: The only time you put in the comma when you have the conjunction is when everything on the left hand side of the comma is an independent clause (sentence) and everything after the conjunction is an independent clause (sentence).

Right: I created a dessert made with honey and butter, and I served it to my class.

Wrong: I created a dessert made with honey and butter, and served it to my class.

<u>and served it to my class</u> is not an independent clause because it isn't a sentence that has a whole thought

<u>I served it to my class</u> is an independent clause because it's a sentence and has a complete thought.

2. Use a comma after an adverb clause that <u>begins</u> the sentence.

Example:

After the lights were turned out, Adam and Gavin sneaked out of bed.

Right: Because Murphy loves us, she leaves a pile of little mouse heads on our door-step every morning.

Wrong: She leaves a pile of little mouse heads on our doorstep every morning, because Murphy seems to love us.

Exercise D
Directions: Correct any comma errors.

1. I revealed your secret to no one but Ajax probably did.

2. Everyone turned to watch Alfred climb out of the study hall window, and run shrieking across the fields.

3. After he discovered 40 feet of sheets tied together Mr. Doolittle began to suspect the boys in the dorm had been climbing out of the window at night.

4. He grabbed his jacket, and he flew out the door.

5. Jane refused to have anything more to do with Ajax, because he accidentally called her "Lisa."

6. Although many people do not believe in the food cravings of pregnant women I was living proof of their power.

7. I skipped the pickles and went right to the ice cream stage.

8. Even though I devoured fifteen ice cream sandwiches a day, I continued to be hungry.

9. For variety, I ate frozen mixed vegetables doused with garlic salt and then came the "sugar attack."

10. I consumed sugar candy by the handfuls and made my tongue orange, green, and raw.

11. I had french fries for breakfast and puff pastries for lunch.

12. I sat on the couch and ate whole loaves of cinnamon bread.

Using Clauses in Your Writing:

1. Add a little variety to your writing by <u>beginning</u> sentences with adverb clauses.

Example: I love Midnight Fudge Bars although I know they're junk food.

Although I know they're junk food, I love Midnight Fudge Bars.

2. Use an adverb clause to <u>combine sentences</u>.

Example: I can begin brushing Murphy's hair.

I pick out the leaves and flowers.

Before I begin brushing Murphy's hair, I pick out the leaves and flowers.

Exercise E

Directions: Combine each of the following groups of sentences by using an adverb clause.

1. I visit my good friend Lolly.
    We always go on a long run together.

    _____

    _____

    _____

2. I found my sweater under the bed.
    I had looked for it all morning.

    _____

    _____

    _____

3. We were watching a very bad movie.
    Someone behind us kept making the most hilarious remarks!

    _____

    _____

    _____

    _____

Clauses and Writing

1.   Subordinate clauses should not be written as sentences.

A subordinate clause by itself is a fragment.

Example: Until the brownies begin to rise. Make sure the oven door stays closed.

until the brownies begin to rise = adverb clause
= fragment

2.   Two independent clauses can't be joined with just a comma.

3.   Two independent clauses can't be joined with nothing in between.

Example: Adam loves fudge brownies, he can eat dozens.

= RUN-ON

Adam loves fudge brownies, and he can eat dozens.

Adam loves fudge brownies he can eat dozens.

= RUN-ON

Adam loves fudge brownies; he can eat dozens.

Exercise F
Directions: Correct any errors.

1.   Although it is 90 degrees outside. Amanda is sleeping under the dresser.

2.   "Bonzo the Great" was terrible it gets my vote for Worst Movie of the Year.

3. The directors turned a potentially hilarious story into a stupid, trashy one, the film had little plot, poor acting, and no action.

4. I thought "Bonzo and Dudley" was a very funny film. Although I did not want to see it at first.

5. Because he got so fat. Barry was put on a diet.

6. He ate three enormous meals a day, then he had a few cans of diet dog food for a snack.

7. One of my favorite topics is "most embarrassing moments," everyone usually has several horrible ones to remember.

8. A truly terrible moment happened to a student of mine, he had been taking magic lessons for several months.

9. When he was with his parents at a Chinese restaurant, He convinced them that he could whisk away the tablecloth. Leaving plates, napkins, and glasses untouched.

10. Before his parents could protest, the boy snapped the tablecloth with a flick of his wrist, he watched in horror as glasses, plates, silverware, and fortune cookies crashed to the floor.

11. How he and his girlfriend smashed their bicycles is another embarrassing story.

12. They were trying to kiss while riding their 10 speeds the spokes locked, the wheels collided, boy, girl, and bikes tumbled to the asphalt.

13. Gavin tried to wake "Murphy the Slug." But it was a hopeless task.

FRAGMENTS AND RUN-ONS

Fragments and Run-Ons

Fragments

We've all been told that a fragment is a part of a sentence, but we need to know what three elements make up a sentence before we can spot fragments.

<u>The 3 essentials to a sentence are:</u>
    1) subject   2) verb   3) complete thought

● Remember that a <u>fragment</u> is <u>missing</u> either a subject, a verb, or a complete thought.

● A complete thought is <u>not</u> necessarily a complement. A complete thought is what is added to the sentence to have it make sense, to make it more of a whole.

● A short sentence is <u>not</u> necessarily a fragment.

Identifying Fragments

The following sentences are really fragments; what are they missing?
1. Murphy and Amanda, my cats.
2. The Dayton School in Ohio.
3. Screaming at the top of his lungs.

One reason we have so much trouble with fragments in our writing seems to be because we <u>talk</u> in fragments all the time.

Example:

1. What are those lumps on the couch?
   Murphy and Amanda, my cats.

2. Where do you go to school?
   The Dayton School in Ohio.

3. What was Adam doing in the closet?
   Screaming at the top of his lungs.

Fragments

Exercise A

Directions: The following sentences are really fragments. Figure out what is missing (subject, verb, or complete thought) and rewrite so that they are complete thoughts.

Example: Chocolate chips, whipped cream, and walnuts. *(needs verb and a complete thought)*

Chocolate chips, whipped cream, and walnuts are in the pie.

1.   One of my worst habits.

_____

_____

2.   After you have baked the angel food cake.

_____

_____

3.   The kitten, trapped in the closet while Amanda watched.

_____

_____

4.   Cruising along in my mini-bike.

_____

_____

5.   Frogs, ants, snakes.

_____

_____

Exercise B

Directions: It's not always necessary to be able to tell specifically what is wrong with a fragment in order to recognize and correct one. After a time, you will develop what grammar books refer to as "sentence sense," which is the ability to know when a sentence "sounds" like a whole, not a fragment. Read the following to yourself. Are they sentences (whole) or fragments (parts)?

1. Poured all the baby powder on the front porch.

2. Hunting, fishing, and playing poker at night.

3. Although Adam loves Midnight Fudge Bars.

4. I have found your missing vampire cape.

5. That is why I no longer eat pepperoni, sausage, and green peppers on my pizza.

6. Amanda is sleeping.

7. Surrounded by all the women he loved.

8. The cats sneak downstairs in the middle of the night.

9. Amanda, her face buried in the whipped cream topping.

10. Devoured the pie that was thawing on the kitchen counter.

Exercise C
Directions: Locate and label any fragments, then change the fragment so it is a sentence.

Example: Underneath Adam's bed /ᶠ, ~~I found broken toys~~
~~and pieces of several puzzles.~~

1. Last Christmas I was very angry with Adam, Gavin, and Trevor. _____
_____

_____

2. Returned from a movie to discover they had eaten two trays of Christmas cookies, a dozen chocolate chip brownies, and ten peppermint sticks. _____
_____

_____

3. Amanda snores. _____
_____

_____

4. Ice cream, french fries, hot dogs, and chili. _____
_____

_____

5. The last time I served Platte County Pie. _____
_____

_____

6. I was disgusted! _____
_____

_____

7. When I moved to Michigan several years ago. _____

_____

_____

8. I forced my cats to become "outdoor" cats. _____

_____

_____

9. They had spent two years living in my apartment in New York. _____

_____

_____

10. They had never been outside before. _____

_____

_____

11. I pushed and shoved Amanda out the door every day. _____

_____

_____

12. Fainted from fright as soon as she got outside. _____

_____

_____

13. Sometimes found her limp body behind a bush, and it was obvious she had fainted again. _____

_____

_____

14. I'll never forget that day! _____

_____

_____

15. Returned from an overnight trip to discover Amanda and Murphy had torn the couch to shreds. _____

_____

_____

16. I refused to let them in the house for days. _____

_____

17. Because I thought of them as "the destroyers." _____

_____

_____

Fragments

Some rules concerning fragments are worth memorizing. Listed below are five fragment rules and some examples that might help you understand them.

1. The "Because" Rule

Most of us have been told by one teacher or another that we should "never begin a sentence with <u>because</u>." They have probably told us this rule because they are afraid we will end up writing a fragment instead of a sentence. However, <u>it is perfectly fine to start a sentence with "because," AS LONG AS WE FINISH OUR THOUGHT.</u>

Example: Because he is weird.   **FRAGMENT**

Because he is weird, I refused to have anything to do with him.   **SENTENCE**

Because he wore a space helmet to school.   **FRAGMENT**

Because he wore a space helmet to school, everyone
thought he was weird.   **SENTENCE**

2. The Conjunction Rule

Try to avoid beginning a sentence with a conjunction. Unlike "because," a conjunction cannot be completed and usually signals the ending of a thought.

Example: We ate pizza and played video games. And then went to see
"The Return of Bonzo" for the fifth time.   **FRAGMENT**

Adam crunched the cookie with his hand, dumped the bowl
of ice cream on the table, and poured milk on his head.
And soon he had the attention of everyone in the cafeteria.   **FRAGMENT**

3. The "For Example" Rule

The expression "for example" may encourage you to write fragments, but it is difficult to say why. Perhaps it is because you may think the phrase makes the sentence sound whole, when in fact it does not. <u>When using the expression "for example," make sure you follow with a verb and complete the thought.</u>

Example: The boy and the father in <u>Incident at Hawk's Hill</u> could not
understand each other. For example, the time when
Ben first met Lobo.   **FRAGMENT**

The boy and the father in <u>Incident at Hawk's Hill</u> could not
understand each other. One example was the time when
Ben first met Lobo.   **SENTENCE**

4. The "Which" Rule

Except when they're asking a question, students should be discouraged from beginning sentences with the word "which" as it tends to result in fragments.

Example: It's almost impossible for me to eat just one cookie.
Which is why I never keep cookies in the house.   **FRAGMENT**

It's almost impossible for me to eat just one cookie,
which is why I never keep them in the house.   **SENTENCE**

5. The Phrases and Clauses Rule

PHRASES are always **FRAGMENTS.**
SUBORDINATE CLAUSES are always **FRAGMENTS.**

Example: Bonzo was in trouble with the principal.
About his science project.

About his science project. = prepositional phrase = **FRAGMENT**

When did the cats eat the hamburger?
During the night.

During the night. = prepositional phrase = **FRAGMENT**

I intercepted Bonzo carrying a tray of dissected frogs. Leaping in front of him.

Leaping in front of him. = participial phrase = **FRAGMENT**

I'd eat Midnight Fudge Bars all day. If I could figure out a way not to gain weight.

If I could figure out a way not to gain weight. = subordinate clause = **FRAGMENT**

I threatened Bonzo with expulsion. Unless he promised to retrieve the dissected frogs he had hidden in the girls' locker room.

Unless he promised to retrieve the dissected frogs he had thrown into the girls' locker room = subordinate clause = **FRAGMENT**

Fragments

Directions: Label the following Ⓕ if it is a fragment and change into a sentence. Label sentences Ⓢ.

1. Amanda snores.

2. When Amanda snores, it drives my husband crazy!

3. Adam played hockey in the garage.

4. Knocked over all the bookcases, boxes, and toys we had stored in the garage.

5. Because it is still raining!

6. Bonzo is incredibly clumsy.

7. For example, leaned back in his chair and crashed to the classroom floor.

8. Which embarrased him so much he tried to pretend he had fallen on purpose.

9. The first time I used a pastry bag.

10. Whipped cream spurted out of the bag and splattered the kitchen walls.

11. But now I am more careful when I use the bag to decorate cakes.

Run-Ons

We know that a sentence has

1) a **Subject**
2) a **Verb**
3) a **Complete Thought**

What is a **Run-On Sentence?**

A <u>run-on sentence</u> is two or more sentences joined

with a comma <u>or</u>

two or more sentences joined with nothing in between.

That's the definition. <u>Length has **NOTHING**</u> to do with run-on sentences. Some very long sentences may be correct, just as some very short sentences may be run-ons.

Example:
Two Sentences Joined With A Comma:
I pleaded with Adam, he just laughed at me.

Run-On

Two Sentences Joined With Nothing In-Between:
I pleaded with Adam he just laughed at me.

Run-On

<u>Correcting run-on sentences:</u>
1.   Use a period between sentences   .
2.   Use a semi-colon between sentences if ideas are closely related   ;
3.   Use a comma and a conjunction between two sentences   **, and**
                                                                                                         , or
                                                                                                         , nor
                                                                                                         , for
                                                                                                         , but

4.   Rewrite the sentences.

Correcting run-on sentences:

      1. **Period**
      2. **Semi-Colon**
      3. **Comma** and **Conjunction**
      4. **Rewriting**

Example:

I opened the ice box door Murphy jumped inside.

1. I opened the ice box door. Murphy jumped inside.
2. I opened the ice box door; Murphy jumped inside.
3. I opened the ice box door, and Murphy jumped inside.
4. When I opened the ice box door, Murphy jumped inside.

Exercise D
Directions: Correct the run-on sentences below.

1. My dream house will have underground caves and deep pools I will use elevators when I want to go down or come back up to the main house.

2. Some vampires live in crypts, most vampires live in coffins.

3. The dying vampire tried desperately to crawl to his coffin, it was almost daylight he could be burned to a crisp.

4. I felt horribly out of place on my first day of school here I was no longer one of the best, but one of the worst.

5. I never have to do homework I have servants do it for me!

Exercise E

Directions: Figure out if each of the following is a sentence or a run-on sentence. If the sentence is correct, leave it alone; correct run-on sentences.

Example:

The cats ate the chocolate mousse. OK

The cats ate the chocolate mousse. They were buried in   RO
whipped cream when I discovered them.

1.   It takes a long time to make, one of my favorite desserts is a chocolate filled angel food cake.

2.   First, bake an angel food cake.

3.   Carefully cut the cake lengthwise, take off the top, you scoop out an inch of cake, then fill the cake with chocolate and whipped cream.

4.   Place the top of the cake back on, I suggest you frost the cake well.

5.   When you cut the cake open, you will see a chocolate center.

Run-On Sentences

Directions: If you find any run-on sentences, correct them.

1. When you tire of regular spaghetti, you can try a variation called "pasta primavera" this dish is spaghetti topped with a sauce made from butter, garlic, broccoli tips, onions, red peppers, and fried mushrooms.

2. An excellent appetizer can be made from a few simple ingredients usually found in anyone's refrigerator use cheese, mayonnaise, green pepper, ham or chicken.

3. Mix grated cheese with a bit of mayonnaise, add vegetables and meat and spread on a cracker.

4. The whipped cream bought in cans is not "real" whipped cream, it certainly isn't fresh.

5. Some people have difficulty preparing whipped cream.

6. If you remember to chill the bowl and the beaters before starting to whip the cream, you shouldn't have any trouble.

7. Liver is nutritious, it is nauseating as well!

8. Even Adam can prepare a simple meal of fried eggs and vegetables, he melts a tablespoon of butter in a skillet and adds onions and sausage. He tosses in a few eggs when the meat and vegetables are nearly cooked.

9. A simple fruit dessert can be made using blueberries, strawberries, light maple syrup and orange juice.

10. Mix the syrup and orange juice, let the mixture sit overnight, pour the juice over the fresh fruit and top with shredded coconut.

11. Bavarian apple torte is one of the most beautiful and delicious desserts you can make, it is easy and fun to put together.

12. Adam and Gavin plotted the theft of the chocolate chip cookies.

Exercise F
Directions: The following stories have no punctuation, making the paragraphs one gigantic run-on. Place punctuation so there are no run-ons at all. Be careful not to create fragments when you are working on run-ons.

Adam fell in love with the Super Heroes when he was three he made my life miserable he talked me into buying Batman, Superman, and Hulk underwear but he refused to wear any clothes over them one day I found him filling the hub caps of the car with rocks so the car would "sound like a Batmobile" if I heard blocks crashing and bookcases being overturned I knew "The Hulk" had struck again once I found two very angry cats trapped in Adam's toy box the villain was none other than Spiderman who had thrown the cats into a "vault" and spun a "web" around the toy box.

Adam caused me some very embarrasing moments during his Super Hero phase probably the worst was the day at the grocery store we had been in the store for nearly an hour gathering everything from tomatoes to skim milk and arguing about junky cereals finally I was able to cross off the last item on my list and fight for a place in line just as it was almost my turn to check through I realized I had forgotten the cat food I instructed Adam to sit still in the cart I ran off down aisle 9 as I was loading my arms with cans I heard a roar of laughter from the direction of the check-out line I assumed Adam was doing something to entertain the crowd nothing however prepared me for the sight of a naked Adam he had tossed his shirt, pants, and underwear on the floor he was standing up in the cart posing as "The Incredible Hulk."

Exercise G

1.   Write an example of a fragment:

_____

_____

_____

2.   Write an example of a run-on sentence:

_____

_____

_____

3.   Explain the difference between a run-on and a fragment:

_____

_____

_____

Exercise H
Directions: The following sentences, paragraphs, and stories contain fragment and run-on errors. Correct them but don't bother to copy out the exercise. Do your corrections right on the page.

1.   Why are you feeling so horrible today? Because I ate three sandwiches, two pieces of lemon custard pie, and a half a chocolate cake.

2.   Bonzo is an extremely clumsy fellow. For example, tripping over his shoelaces and falling down the stairs.

3.   Because it is still raining!

4.   Although many people eat yogurt because they think it is "diet" food. It actually has as many calories as a serving of ice cream.

5.   However, yogurt is more healthy to eat than ice cream, ice cream may be stuffed with preservatives and sugar.

6.   Did you know oranges are not really "orange"? Most of the oranges we buy in the store have been injected with an orange dye, this is to make them more attractive, so people will buy them.

7.   Most of the beef you eat has been treated with chemicals, cows are injected with chemicals. That make them grow heavy and lean. Instead of heavy and fat. Unless they are free to roam, cows will get fat, they do nothing all day but eat, sleep, and moo.

8.   The best beef in the world comes from grass fed cows. That have been allowed to graze.

When I heard the door slam. I knew Adam had locked himself in the bathroom again, I ran upstairs and pounded on the door. But he wouldn't let me in. I pleaded with him. But he just laughed at me. The sound of running water panicked me I could hear fiendish chuckles behind the door. When I heard Adam ripping open a box, I knew he was planning to pour all his "Mr. Bubble" in the bathtub I pounded on the door again but was ignored within a few minutes soapy water started to seep from underneath the door.

Adam was, at times, a difficult child. He threw his shoes in the toilet, decorated the kitchen wall with finger paints, he complained he couldn't slip through the doors like Casper the ghost, and he stuffed all my good silverware down the heating grates. When I was ready to stuff <u>him</u> down the heating grate, I reminded myself that I was lucky things could be worse. He could be Elizabeth Radler. Elizabeth was, in my estimation, the worst three year old in the United States, the only child I ever knew who was expelled from nursery school. Elizabeth smiled at people sweetly. But she would lean down and bite arms as hard as she could. She scratched, kicked, spit, she threw food. And locked her cats, dogs, and baby brother in the closet. Adam had his bad moments, none were as bad as Elizabeth's.

The week-long rain had ended but the grass trees and air were still heavy with moisture classes had let out for the day and the two students were squeaking through the heavy grass of the lower fields one marching ahead of the other they stopped at the bridge crossing the lagoon which wound its way around the nearby homes the water was boiling swelling free after months of winter captivity the kids draped their arms over the bridge railing and watched the leaves moss and old cakes of ice swirl by they noticed a large mass rounding the bend floating cumbersomely along the kids ran to the edge of the lagoon and poked at the mass as it bumped along the bank their sticks prodded the bundle until the youngest boy reached for one end and the thing turned over.

I can't stand the smell or sight of liver. Because of Bill Panek who sat in front of me during the first four grades of elementary school, we were forced to sit at our desks for lunch. And Bill always sat right in front of me. Each day he unpacked his paper bag, took out an enormous piece of raw liver wrapped in wax paper. He munched happily; licking the liver blood from the paper.

FREQUENT ERRORS

Frequent Errors

Part One

1. a~~lot~~

There is no such word!

<u>A lot</u> is two words.

 It's better to avoid this expression completely or substitute another phrase, as in:

 I love chocolate.

 I like chocolate very much.

2. any~~w~~ays

There is no such word!

The word you should use is <u>anyway</u>.

3. <u>accept, except</u>

<u>accept</u>: to receive; to give your o.k.;
   to answer yes; to agree with

 I can't accept that ridiculous excuse for an explanation.

 Bonzo was accepted at Froggy Prep, Nerd Academy, and Space Cadet School.

 Please accept my invitation to dinner; we are having stuffed clams, baked shrimp, and bay scallops with lemon butter.

<u>except</u>: the exception; everyone or everything <u>but</u>

 All the boys ate chili dogs, cotton candy, and greasy popcorn except Fred.

 All the boys rode the Whirlwind and the Hurricane except Fred.

 All the boys got sick except Fred.

4.   <u>can, may</u>

   <u>can</u>: something physically possible; a possibility

      Can five eighth grade boys fling Bonzo out of the gym?

      Can you scale the wall in the yard?

      Can you eat more fudge bars and cupcakes than Fred?

   <u>may</u>: asking permission

      May I finish the rest of the chocolate cream pie?

      May I be excused from the study hall?

5.   <u>could/of, should/of, would/of are always incorrect</u>

   could <u>have</u>   should <u>have</u>   would <u>have</u>

         have
      We could of beaten that football team, but our key player was ill.

         have
      I should of eaten an apple instead of chocolate chips.

         have
      Sally would of kissed Bonzo, but she couldn't catch him.

6.   <u>etc.</u>, <u>ect.</u>

   The correct abbreviation for et cetera is <u>etc</u>.
   ect. - doesn't exist and is never correct

7. <u>good</u> and <u>well</u>

    <u>good</u>: used as an adjective

    A <u>good</u> sauce for ice cream can be made with chocolate and peanut butter.
    adj.   noun

    <u>well</u>: used as an adverb

    I did <u>well</u> on the algebra quiz.
    v. adv.

    Rule: Never use the expression "did good"!

    You can never "do" anything good, only <u>well</u>.

8. <u>hole, whole</u>

    <u>hole</u>: a tear, space, or opening

    There's a hole in his new polo shirt.

    Adam stabbed a hole in his Bonzo Punch Bag.

    <u>whole</u>: the entire; not cut up or divided

    Amanda and Murphy ate the whole pie.

    The whole class is invited to my house for chocolate cream fudge cake.

9. <u>know, no, now</u>

    <u>know</u>: knowledge

    Adam knows Dracula lurks outside the door every night.

    We know how Bonzo feels about socks.

    <u>no</u>: none

    There will be no raisin cake for you, Bonzo!

    <u>now</u>: time

    Now is the perfect time to sneak downstairs and eat the rest of the lemon mousse.

10. <u>like</u>

<u>like</u>: use the word to make a comparison or as a verb.

Bonzo wants his hair cut like John's.

I like Peter's whiffle haircut, but he is more handsome with long hair.

<u>AVOID</u> overusing the word <u>like</u> in your conversation, as in:

"Hey, like you know, it's like, well, like there was this guy and he like took this car and like he thought the garage door was open, but it wasn't so he like..."

Exercise A
Directions: Examine the underlined words. If the word is used correctly, leave it the way it is. If the word is used incorrectly, cross it out and make the correction.

                       have
Example: I <u>should of</u> used <u>a lot</u> more vanilla in the sauce.

1. <u>Can</u> we go to the park <u>anyways</u>?

2. The <u>whole</u> class <u>knows</u> of the "secret" romance.

3. Trevor listened intently to Adam's explanation as to why he should eat the donut <u>hole</u> and leave the rest for Adam.

4. A well-stocked kitchen should have the following items: fresh spices, a set of good knives, fine cookbooks, <u>ect.</u>

5. The team played <u>good</u> <u>except</u> for a few fumbles.

Exercise B

Directions: Read the following sentences carefully. If you find a mistake, make the correction.

1. The whole menu that we had planned was unexceptable.

2. I thought Adam had done a good job of cleaning up his room until I discovered all his toys stuffed under the bed!

3. "Winston tastes good like a cigarette should."

4. Can I please finish the rest of the ice cream sundae pie?

5. No spaghetti sauce is prepared as well as the one Diane makes.

11. like/when

Like when is a phrase that should not be used when trying to present an example. The phrase is grammatically unsound and also encourages the use of fragments in writing.

Incorrect: Gavin and Adam often get into trouble when they are together. Like when they locked Trevor in the bathroom and told him Dracula was in there with him.

Substitute "for example" or rewrite the sentences to avoid use of "like when."

Gavin and Adam often get into trouble when they are together. For example, one day they locked Trevor in the bathroom and told him Dracula was in there with him.

Gavin and Adam get into trouble when they are together. Once they locked Trevor in the bathroom and told him Dracula was in there with him.

12. <u>LY on adverbs</u>

<u>ly</u> should be added to certain adverbs:

Dracula captured me because I ran slow.

                                v. adv.

Dracula captured me because I ran slow<u>ly</u>.

                                v. adv.

13. <u>than, then</u>

<u>than</u>: used when making choices or comparisons

    I'd rather eat chocolate mousse <u>than</u> raw liver.

                mousse   <u>or</u>   liver

    It's better to be short <u>than</u> tall.

           short <u>or</u> tall

<u>then</u>: used in relationship to time or the passing of time; usually meaning "what is going to happen next"

    First soak the raisins in water, <u>then</u> add the mixture to the peeled oranges and ripe berries.

    The vampire begged to be let in, <u>then</u> he hypnotized me with his gruesome red eyes.

14. their, there, they're

their: used to show possession of a thing

This pile of junk is their mess.

It wasn't difficult for them to finish their desserts.

there: a place; a word placed before a verb

Adam stuffed his clothes and shoes in the cubby over there.

There is a small piece of blueberry pie left on the counter.

they're: the contraction for "they are"

They're planning to serve strawberries and ice cream for dessert.

They are planning to serve strawberries and ice cream for dessert.

I suppose they're placing the garlic wreath on the door to discourage vampires.

I suppose they are placing the garlic wreath on the door to discourage vampires.

15. threw, through

threw: an action, usually of the arm!

Adam threw his blocks out the bedroom window and smacked Mr. Cox on the head.

The ninth grade boys threw the football down the hall and watched in dismay as it bounced off the teacher's head.

through: passing, traveling, moving; to finish with

Walk through these doors to reach the other classroom.

The boys sneaked through hallways as quietly as possible; they didn't want to wake up the dorm master.

I hope we get through *A Tale of Two Cities* soon; I can't cope with the French Revolution for another week.

16. <u>to, too, two</u>

<u>to</u>: used as a preposition or an infinitive (verb)

It's time <u>to</u> go <u>to</u> the beach.

The boys decided <u>to eat</u> as many sandwiches as they could.

Please give us directions <u>to</u> Dracula's castle.

<u>too</u>: used as an adverb to show degrees of something; or means "also"

It's <u>too</u> difficult to climb out of the third story window.

I ate <u>too</u> much of the chocolate cream pie.

"I want to go, <u>too</u>!" shouted Trevor as Adam and Gavin raced to the soccer field.

<u>two</u>: 2

The <u>two</u> boys convinced Trevor to make the beds and clean the room.

The <u>two</u> pies were made with raisins and chocolate.

17. <u>weather, whether</u>

<u>weather</u>: rain, sun, clouds, etc.

<u>whether</u>: used in choices or possibilities

It doesn't matter <u>whether</u> we go or stay.
               choice: go <u>or</u> stay

Ask your mother <u>whether</u> you can go to the concert.
          possibility: go to the concert <u>or</u> not

NOTE: Avoid the expression "whether or not." The word <u>whether</u> includes all possibilities — going <u>or</u> not.

18. your, you're

your: used to show possession

Your paper on the book sounds like the jacket cover!

"Please, Adam, stop drawing on your legs with that marker."

you're: the contraction for "you are"

I suppose you're planning to draw elephants on Trevor's legs again.

I suppose you are planning to draw elephants on Trevor's legs again.

You're simply not going to ride that bike into the pool.

You are simply not going to ride that bike into the pool.

19. wear, where, were

wear: using clothing or articles on your person

Don't wear this shirt; Adam and Gavin have drawn spaceships on the back.

where: referring to a place

Where have you hidden the cats?

were: a verb

Where were you planning to sneak off to before I caught you?

Adam and Gavin were trying to tie baby booties to the kitten's paws.

20. which, witch, wich

which: what one

Which do you prefer, the chocolate fudge cake or plum pie?

"Which one of you stabbed Trevor with the plastic sword?"

witch: brooms, Halloween

wich: no such word!

21. write, right

write: to make letters or words

"Please, Trevor, don't write your name on the bookcase again."

right: a direction; the correct way

Take a right turn by the yellow sign and you will have reached the school.

Trevor always has his shoes on the wrong foot because he can't tell his left from his right foot.

The right way to make this spaghetti sauce is to make sure the tomatoes are ripe, the spices fresh, and the olive oil very rich.

Most Frequent Errors

Directions: Make corrections if necessary.

1.   "Are we, like dismissed?"

2.   Everyone excepted the invitation except Bonzo.

3.   Alot of people do not care for soap operas.

4.   I should of bought a bike like Arthur's.

5.   Can you reach the books on the high shelf?

6.   It's too difficult to finish that project anyways.

7.   The karate teacher was pleased that Adam did so good during his first lesson.

Directions: Answer the following questions:

1. Which is correct — etc. or ect.?

2. Which word is used when asking permission — may or can?

3. Which word means something physically possible — can or may?

4. Which is used as an adjective — well or good?

5. When is the word "like" acceptable?

Directions: Use each of the following words in sentences. Use and spell them correctly. Try using more than one word in the same sentence.

accept _____

_____

except _____

_____

can _____

_____

may _____

_____

good _____

_____

well _____

_____

whole _____

_____

hole _____

_____

than   _____

         _____

then   _____

         _____

their   _____

         _____

there   _____

         _____

they're _____

         _____

to   _____

         _____

too   _____

         _____

weather _____

         _____

whether _____

         _____

your   _____

         _____

you're   _____

         _____

write   _____

         _____

right   _____

         _____

Exercise C
Directions: Examine the underlined word. If the word is used correctly, just leave it; make the correction if necessary.

1. If <u>your</u> getting <u>too</u> bored with plain chocolate chip cookies, you might try spreading the dough in a pan and covering with chocolate sauce and coconut.

2. <u>Their</u> are several ways <u>to</u> make good spaghetti sauce, but the best is to start with fresh plum tomatoes, onions, green peppers, and basil.

3. <u>Wich</u> of you boys encouraged Trevor to climb into the clothes hamper?

4. My husband chased Murphy around the house, <u>than</u> he threatened jokingly <u>to</u> make her "go for a ride in the blender."

5. Trevor <u>threw</u> his army figures, a plastic snake, and a box of crayons in his bath water.

Exercise D
Directions: Make corrections where necessary.

1. When the whether is hot, the cats squish themselves against the window screens and sleep all day.

2. Too much television viewing will turn your brain into oatmeal.

3. There are almost no natural or real ingredients in some cupcakes; the spongy cake is made complete from chemicals, and the "whipped cream" filling is nothing more then food coloring, glue, and artificial sweeteners.

4. Dracula was whering a beautiful black silk cape and a thin bow tie.

5. Amanda likes to sleep on top of my head.

Most Frequent Errors

Directions: Circle the correct word.

1.   I ate (alot, a lot) of ice cream sandwiches when I was pregnant.

2.   I figured I was going to get fat (anyway, anyways), so I continued to eat as much as I could.

3.   I (accepted, excepted) the fact that I would have to gain some weight when I was pregnant.

4.   "I (can, may) lose whatever weight I gain," I thought to myself when I was pregnant.

5.   I should (of, have) had more sense (than, then) that!

6.   I ate ice cream sandwiches, frozen vegetables, eclairs, chocolates, (ect., etc.)

7.   I also did a (good, well) job of polishing off all the crackers and bread in the house.

8.   I ate extremely (well, good) at dinnertime, (too, to).

9.   It was, like one of the dumbest things I ever did when I like, gained, like fifty pounds when I was, like pregnant.

*   *   *   *   *   *   *   *   *   *   *

Are the following underlined words used correctly or incorrectly? If there are mistakes, correct them.

1.   I ate <u>frequently</u> and <u>continuous</u>.

2.   I would rather eat potato skins <u>than</u> liver.

3. <u>To</u> make a delicious cheesecake, first soften some cream cheese, <u>then</u> add eggs. You should add whipped cream, <u>to</u>.

4. <u>There</u> planning a dessert party for <u>your</u> school! Please make sure <u>they're</u> planning <u>to</u> include <u>you're</u> class, <u>too</u>.

5. If the <u>wheather</u> is warm, I won't make chocolate mousse. Why? If it is <u>too</u> hot, it is <u>to</u> difficult to whip the egg whites necessary for a mousse.

Frequent Errors

Part Two: Apostrophes; Capitalization; Spelling

I.   Apostrophes

A. used for <u>contractions</u>, taking the place of the missing letter or letters

I can't stand it when my friend eats raw hamburger.

I cannot stand it when my friend eats raw hamburger.

B. used for showing <u>possession</u>

Pasta primavera is <u>James'</u> special Italian dish.

Amanda's guilty look made me suspect she had shoved Murphy off the balcony.

Common Mistakes With Apostrophes:

A. a common mistake is to place an apostrophe on a plural noun:

Thanks for all the get-well card's.   **incorrect**

Thanks for all the get-well cards.   **correct**

B. another common mistake is misplacing the apostrophe when referring to one or more person

(one boy)   The boy's room was filled with junk. **correct**

(two or more boys)   The boys' room was filled with junk. **correct**

Rules: — if two or more people involved = s'
— ask yourself: do I need the apostrophe for possession or a contraction?
If not, **NO** apostrophe

Exercise E
Directions: Make corrections if necessary:

1. Amandas fur is falling out.

2. Its easy to make your own pizza, but it is very expensive to do so.

3. This Thanksgiving my mother is going to baste the turkey with a coffee liqueur. The rich flavoring seeps' into the meat; its delicious!

4. Adams' favorite toy's are his building blocks and Boston Bruins' record.

5. When we plan the party, let's keep in mind that there are a dozen frozen cream fudge pies in the refrigerator for dessert.

Exercise F
Directions: Rewrite the sentence so the people (or cats) possess a noun. Use apostrophes correctly.

Example: the room belonging to Adam and Gavin
Adam's and Gavin's room is a disaster!

1. the toys belonging to Trevor and his brothers

   _____

   _____

   _____

   _____

2. the piece of chicken stolen by Edna, Amanda, and Murphy

   _____

   _____

   _____

   _____

3. the broken pencils, chewed up textbooks, and forty Tarzan books belonging to Bonzo are stored in his schoolroom desk

   _____

   _____

   _____

   _____

Exercise G

Directions: The following words can be used as plural nouns <u>or</u> as words showing possession. Write two sentences for each word, 1. one sentence using the word as a plural noun, 2. the other using the word as a possessive.

Example: Saturday

possessive ▶ 1. Saturday's football game will be held at home, not away.

plural ▶   2. Adam likes to spend his Saturdays playing soccer and baseball with his friend, Leigh.

1. stereo

_____

_____

_____

2. cake

_____

_____

_____

3. vampire

_____

_____

_____

4. school

_____

_____

_____

5. concert

_____

_____

_____

Apostrophes

Directions: The following sentences contain no words with apostrophes. Should they? If you find a mistake, make the correction.

1. The students should stop teasing the teachers.

2. Elegant chocolate desserts add a great deal to a delicious meal.

3. The two cats violent tempers often clash.

4. The hair on Bonzos head is nearly gone after a skirmish with an electric razor.

5. Frustrated with the study of grammar usage, Bonzo slammed his fists on the flimsy desk top and broke it into several pieces.

Directions: The following sentences contain words with apostrophes. In fact, all letters ending in "s" have apostrophes. Should they? If you find a mistake, make the correction.

1. Bonzo's sense of humor causes' laughs', hysterics', and adult despair.

2. The faculty room is always' littered with half-empty coffee cups', rumpled newspapers', and exhausted teachers'.

3. The teacher's desk was piled high with compositions' and reports'. (**one teacher**)

4. The students' party will be held at the headmaster's house. (**all students**)

5. When asked what he wanted for birthday presents', Adam replied, "two toy stores'."

Correct Use of Apostrophes

Directions: Choose the word in the parentheses that uses the apostrophe correctly.

1. (Cindys', Cindy's) room is cluttered with school books, posters, and candy wrappers.

2. That (schools', school's) dress code is very strict!

3. The three (boys', boy's) clothes were torn during the scuffle in the hall.

4. The (Colbys', Colby's) house was painted over the weekend.

5. The (teachers', teacher's) room was filled with boxes of used books.

Directions: Can you find any apostrophe errors? Correct them if you do.

1. The boys' crowded into the kitchen and were ready for their teachers cooking lesson.

2. Hughs' eggs' slipped from his hands and landed in a gooey mess on the floor.

3. Brian's and Tony's feet slid soggily through the yellow goo on the floor.

4. Andrew's chocolate chip pie was delicious!

5. The cakes' made by Josh and Whit were rising in the oven.

6. The three cakes' frosting were made from butter and chocolate.

Frequent Errors

II. Capitalization

<u>capitals</u>: used for proper names or the beginning of sentences

> Errors in capitalization are usually due to carelessness rather than misunderstanding of the rules!

III. Spelling

The following words are frequently misspelled:

1. beginning
2. experience
3. dye: to color
4. die: death
5. dying: process of death
6. believe
7. does, doesn't
8. sense
9. since: because
10. piece, peice: a part of something
11. clothes: what you wear

Most Frequent Errors

Directions: If you find a mistake, correct it.

1. Adam dosen't really beleive in vampires', but he is afraid of my stories anyways.

2. Don't ever try to die youre hair!

3. Sence you have been so well behaved, lets splurge and buy a pound of chocolates'!

4. In the begining of my latest vampire story, Draculas coffin is stolen and sneaked into the gym.

5.   Adam through a glass a orange juice at the cats.

6.   I should of made the truffle cake because this cake was to difficult.

7.   Ive hidden Adam's halloween candy because he keeps asking for chocolates and pea-
     nuts' for breakfast.

8.   They're several delicious recipes for chicken, but one of my favorites' involves soak-
     ing the chicken in cooking sherry and onions overnight.

9.   Alot of people do not care for spicy mexican food, but I love it!

10. Because it is often difficult to find good mexican food products, my parents send me
     Pinto Beans, tamale husks', and jalapeño peppers from colorado.

Exercise H

Directions: The following sentences contain a variety of errors; correct where necessary.

1.   Theres a chance well have a chocolate cake for our first class party.

2.   Although it's very easy to make, key lime pie might be too rich for youre taste!

3.   Thier is another recipe Im thinking of trying, but the beginning steps are quite difficult.

4.   Adam is very fond of double chocolate brownies'.

5.   The more experience I have in the kitchen, the easier cooking becomes.

6.   I would of made an apple spice cake for you, but I didn't have enough nutmeg.

7.   For you're party, lets make a chocolate honey nut torte, an almond glazed pie, and a
     truffle cake.

8. All of us did so poor at our first cooking lesson that we couldn't eat what we had made.

9. Their whole team will take the bus to the game.

10. Adam dose not like what he calls "bits." Sprinkles on ice cream are considered "bits", so are peppers, mushrooms, and sausage.

11. If you dont use enough water when boiling spaghetti, alot of sticky film will be left on the cooked pasta.

12. When he could no longer stand her snoring, Mr. Southworth through Amanda out of the house into a pile of snow.

13. Of all the Thanksgiving dinners' I've prepared, this year's was the worst. I'd been baking and cooking all day. Finally, it was dinnertime. As soon as we sat down at the table, Murphy leaped on the sideboard where several lit candles were burning and set her tail on fire.

14. This could of been delicious clam chowder, but it had too much ground pepper.

15. Whether you eat the last peice of pie doesn't matter to me.

16. I wish I had excepted your advice abut dating that awful boy.

17. We played a good game.

18. We played good against our rivals.

19. No kid should be eating chocolate covered cereal with chocolate milk, anyways.

20. Which cat is sleeping inside the mattress?

21. When their asked to clean up their rooms, Adam and Gavin hide in the closet.

22. When I was in high school, I tried to dye my hair blond but it turned out a flaming red color.

23. Her yelling doesn't affect me.

24. Her yelling doesn't have any effect on me.

Most Frequent Errors

Directions: Correct errors in punctuation, spelling, capitalization, and usage.

1. I should of done good on the math test because I studied very hard.

2. Alot of students find word problems to difficult to understand at first.

3. Can you bring your bicycle, too?

4. I can bring everything accept the electric football game.

5. Our lakeside picnic will include roast beef sandwiches, mounds of potato salad, hot dogs, ect.

6. I know potato chips will like, you know, complement the hole meal.

7. I enjoy traveling with my students. Like when a group of us visited New York City last spring.

8. Saute the scallops' slow in a buttered pan, than add the mushrooms.

9. Its better to use small amounts of common sense than large quantities of bravery.

10. Wich book are youre students interested in reading?

11. There only intrigued with the begining of the story.

12. It may be difficult to beleive, but spring will be here soon.

13. Each school year is an experience.

14. When my father could not longer stand his childrens constant television viewing, he through the TV off a hill.

15. Their is another novel im considering reading, but the beginning of the book is too difficult and confusing.

Most Frequent Errors

Directions: If you find a mistake, correct it.

1. The kind of chocolate mousse you create depends on you're mood. If you like a light, fluffy dessert, use less chocolate; if your feeling decadent, use more chocolate.

2. A lot of people have difficulty when there trying to cook a turkey for the first time. The bird turns out burned, tasteless or to dry.

3. You could of substituted Bonzos chocolate for this recipe, but Swiss chocolate is better and tastes extremely good.

4. Too make chocolate torte, it is necessary to have the write ingredients: raisins, almonds, melted Swiss chocolate, ect.

5. After you finished gathering the ingredients, stir together and than pour into a buttered baking pan.

6. I threw the uncompleted grammar book across the room.

7. I slammed the oven door and through the partially cooked liver and onions across the kitchen.

8. Smack! The mess smashed into the wall and slid slow to the floor.

9. When the whether was good, Adam loaded his red wagon with toys' and blankets and "ran away."

10. When Adam cant decide wich shirt to where, he dosen't wear any at all.